"Rita Losee is on a mission to wake us up to our possibilities. She has met incredible challenges head-on and emerged with joy—so can you! Read this book and find your magic!"
Brian D. Biro, Author
Beyond Success and *The Joyful Spirit*

"This book is a must for any person seeking to grow personally and professionally and become more productive. Rita Losee has insights and ideas that can really make a difference. I strongly recommend this provocative and positive book."
Bill Gove, First President of the National Speakers Association
Cavett Award Winner

"This book is awesome! Rita has done a terrific job and I'm confident if you invest the time to read it you will receive a lifetime of benefit."
Ray Pelletier, Author
Permission to Win

UNLOCK *Your* Possibilities

How to Stop Shooting Yourself Down and Selling Yourself Short

Dr. Rita H. Losee

Summer Books

Unlock Your Possibilities: How to Stop Shooting Yourself Down and Selling Yourself Short Copyright ©1998 by Pontalba Press. Printed and bound in the United States of America. All rights reserved. No part of this book may be reproduced in any form or by any electronic or mechanical means including information storage and retrieval systems without permission in writing from the publisher, except by a reviewer, who may quote brief passages in a review. Published by Summer Books, an imprint of Pontalba Press, 4417 Dryades Street, New Orleans, Louisiana, 70115.

Excerpt from *Women Who Run With the Wolves* by Clarissa Pinkola Estés, Ph.D., Copyright © 1992, 1995. All rights reserved. Reprinted by kind permission of Dr. Estés and Ballantine Books, a division of Random House, Inc.

Excerpts from the article "Report Card for Americans' Eating Habits" reprinted by kind permission of Tufts University *Health & Nutrition Letter.*

Permission to quote from *Awaken the Giant Within: How to Take Immediate Control of Your Mental, Emotional, Physical, and Financial Destiny* by Anthony J. Robbins is hereby granted by Brad N. Hunsaker on behalf of Anthony J. Robbins.

Excerpts from *Healthy, Wealthy and Wise: Fundamentals of Workplace Health Promotion* reprinted by kind permission of Wellness Councils of America.

Permission to quote from the works of Brian Tracy has been granted.

First Edition

Edited by Winter C.R. Neil and Sandra S. Chaisson
Designed by Stephanie Stephens
Author Photograph courtesy of Michael Miller, On Location Studio of Photography

Losee, Rita H.
    Unlock your possibilities : how to stop shooting yourself down and selling yourself short / Rita H. Losee. – 1st ed.
    p. cm.
    ISBN: 1-891643-00-2

    1. Self-esteem.   2. Self-help techniques.   3. Weight loss – Psychological aspects.   I. Title.

BF697.5.S46L67 1998   158.1
          QBI98-417

To the memory of Judy Flannery, a magnificent woman who personified the lessons of this book.

To the women of Hodder House Mentoring Program, Massachusetts Prison and the courage they display in learning those same lessons.

Warning: This book could change your life!

ACKNOWLEDGEMENTS

Until now I have never understood why Oscar winners stand on the podium and gush, "I want to thank…and…and…" until the viewers are all longing for a commercial. Now I do. There is a bright ribbon that weaves in, around, and through the totality of my life. It is the presence of other people who have shared in some way on my life's journey. I could not have written this book if any of them had been absent from the casting call of my life—and thus I owe heartfelt gratitude to them all.

Some of those people have been supportive and affirming. Some of them have been frustrating and triggered anger, pain, and dismay in me. Others challenged me to keep growing and some hated it when I did. Some built me up and some let me down. Some loved me and embraced me—others did not. But, all of them enriched me. And as I sit at my computer on a murky March day, I want to acknowledge each of them individually. I want them all to know how *vital* they are to my life. I want them to feel acknowledged by me. I want them to know that I am deeply grateful for the experience—all of it. I want them to know how much I love them and that love is the most powerful force in the Universe. Different experiences would have created a different Rita and…I love who I am and what I am doing.

Particular thanks go to:

The people around the campfires at Down Point.

My Heinlein collection.

My colleagues, mentors, and friends from the National Speakers Association.

The wonderful team at Pontalba Press who transformed a rough draft into a book.

My sons who have taught me much and brought great joy to my life.

Table of Contents

INTRODUCTION .... *xiii*

CHAPTER 1
Disconnection and Dis-ease *1*

CHAPTER 2
What You Knew When You Were Two: Uncovering,
Recovering, or Discovering Self *17*

CHAPTER 3
Making Friends with Discipline *31*

CHAPTER 4
Taking Stock, the First Step in Taking Charge of Your Life *43*

CHAPTER 5
Coming to Your Senses: Staying in Your Right Mind *59*

CHAPTER 6
Creating a Mission Statement for Your Life *75*

CHAPTER 7
Learning to Live in the Skinny Branches *91*

CHAPTER 8
Fit and Fabulous! Putting More Life in Your Lifestyle *107*

CHAPTER 9
Address Your Stress: Getting Cool, Calm and Connected *123*

CHAPTER 10
The MotivACTion Plan: How to Get What You Want *139*

CHAPTER 11
Chickens Don't Fly: Get Off Your DUFF—
Doubt, Uncertainty, Fear, Failure *153*

CHAPTER 12
Integrate—Don't Disintegrate *171*

Introduction

AS A VERY YOUNG WOMAN, I sat in a darkened theater in New York watching a production of *Auntie Mame*. In one scene Mame stood still at center stage, thrust out her arms and bellowed, "I want to live!" In the back of that theatre my heart echoed back, "Me, too, me, too." And so I have been living and simultaneously learning about life. *Unlock Your Possibilities* was being written as I lived, although I wasn't conscious that my life was shaping a book. What I was trying to do was live the best life I could live. I was also trying to "play the game by the rules." What I came to realize was that in order to live the best life I could live, I needed to carefully examine "the rules," determine if they made sense to me and if they were the correct rules, and then create my own rules for living my own life.

I remember my mother trilling William Shakespeare when I was a child: "This above all, to thine own self be true." She doesn't remember repeating the quote. I do, so the words obviously struck a chord within me. They spoke to my own inherent recognition of a basic truth about how to live a successful, fulfilled life. What my experiences have revealed to me is that it's difficult to be true to thine "own self."

In order to do that, I have to first know who and what my "self" is. The beliefs, thoughts, and perceptions that constitute "self" are woven like the individual strands of a piece of wool yarn. It's difficult to pick out individual strands. It's also difficult to pick out our own belief strands without getting them mixed up with the beliefs of parents, teachers, siblings, religious leaders, rock stars, or historical figures. An essential part of the journey to becoming the glorious self we were meant to be is willingness to go back and search through the tangled threads of our own lives and beliefs and separate out what it is that we believe from what "they" believe. Integrity will then require that we act out of our beliefs.

Every human who has ever lived has been unique. We all have the capacity to define, refine, and develop ourselves so that we are the best possible expression of that potential. We all have unique gifts that only we can give expression to. And if we don't choose to unlock our possibilities and develop our gifts, neither the world nor we will realize the benefit of those gifts. Sometimes when I am speaking, audience members will tell me that they'd like to be like me. I tell them, "No, don't try to be like me. Choose aspects of me that resonate for you but use them not to be like me, but to be like you. Be the best *you* you can be."

Because this is an autobiographical self-help book, friends and relatives appear in its pages. I could not write this book without telling the truth—as I see the truth—about my experiences. If other participants in my life see the same situations from a different perspective, that's okay. All of us filter the events of our lives through our own hearts and minds. It would be impossible for them to see situations from my perspective.

I wrote from the understanding that the people I have "done life" with, have all made contributions to the experience that I call "my life." They have generally been/are people of integrity and good will, people of courage, and people seeking their own understanding. They mirror aspects of me as I do them. They are not perfect (that's a mirror, too). They made "mistakes" or at least have done things that I label mistakes. Another mirror. They have greatly enriched the experience of my life and I have come to the wisdom of seeing it as all good. We can all accept the sacred individuality of each of us.

Some of the opinions that I express within this book may stimulate you, upset you, anger you, disturb you, and/or perplex you. I hope so! I'd hate to think I wrote a boring book. That aside, if you are reacting to my words, creative energy is being released. Einstein said, "The thinking that has brought me this far has created some problems that this thinking cannot solve." If there are problems/opportunities in your life that your thinking has caused, you need new thinking. One definition of insanity is doing the same old thing and expecting different results. So, an emotional reaction to what I have said is a sign of Life, a signal that the Creative Force of the Universe is flowing through you. That's wonderful. I can think of no better result than that my words are useful in creating Life flow. My fondest wish for this book is that it ignite sparks in the lives of its readers.

The butterfly on the cover has special significance for me. In China butterflies are symbols of joy. We should all live surrounded by joy. We are all butterflies. Our authentic selves are wrapped in the hard, brown dryness of the cocoons of our beliefs. Inside the butterfly cocoons exists great beauty which Mother Nature will follow a step-by-step process to release into the world. Inside of each of us, too, rests a creature of exquisite beauty and capacity. To the best of my knowledge, butterflies aren't given the choice whether to realize their beauty—the process simply unfolds. As humans, we *are* given a choice; we can stay wrapped and confined in the darkness, or we can choose to break out and fly free.

Another aspect of the Monarch butterfly that resonates for me is the fact that they live in New England during the summer and winter in Mexico. Those delicate-appearing, fabulously beautiful creatures are paragons of power, direction, and stamina. If it is possible for a butterfly to fly thousand of miles for its place in the sun, then surely it is possible for me to follow my own path to my destiny in the sun. Fly free!

Chapter 1
DISCONNECTION AND DIS-EASE

IT WAS MIDNIGHT when I stepped out of the hut 17,000 feet up on the slopes of Mt. Kilimanjaro. The night sky blazed with billions of stars crystallized by the cold, clear air. A full moon added a softer light to the scene. The only sounds were the quiet murmur of multiple languages and the crunch of our boots on the rocky soil. Soon I would be embarking on the summit attempt. A German traveler from another party pointed out the Southern Cross to me, my first sight of a constellation that had fascinated me since I was a child. I shivered from cold and anticipation. What would it be like? Could I do it? Did I have the stamina and endurance to achieve the goal of standing on top of Kilimanjaro?

We moved toward the trail which quickly became very steep and rose in a series of endless switchbacks. Our progress was slow as we labored in the thin air. I was dizzy from the lack of oxygen. The Tylenol I was taking every four hours to relieve my altitude-induced headache was no longer effective. Occasionally the quiet conversation of the guides, speaking words we did not understand, broke the cold silence of the night.

Throughout the night we climbed. Several people decided to turn back and descend to the hut. Each climber was escorted back to the hut by a guide who then re-climbed the slope that was challenging every cell in my body. Totally engrossed in the task of continued upward movement, I kept my eyes on the heels of George's boots. When his left foot moved, my left foot moved. When his right foot moved, my right foot moved. Locking my mind onto the rhythm of his foot movement induced a semi-hypnotic state which lessened the effort I needed to make. I coached myself to breathe. "Breathe as deeply as you can, Rita. Get every little bit of oxygen you can from each breath." My conscious awareness was limited to breathing and the effort of keeping *my feet moving.*

At 5:30 A.M., we were at Gilman Point at the edge of the crater that crowns Mt. Kilimanjaro. It felt so good to rest! Some members of the group decided to descend. I was not the least bit interested in descending...the summit was so near. Soon I would stand on the summit of Mt. Kilimanjaro. Six of us resumed our climb. Now the trail was snow-covered as it curved along the edge of the crater's rim. We were only a few vertical feet below the summit, traversing terrain that consisted of a series of gently rising hills. But gently rising hills at over 19,000 feet are hills of another effort. To pace myself, I devised the strategy of counting off fifty paces and then stopping to rest, leaning on my walking stick. Once again, my awareness was limited to breathing, moving one foot in front of the other, and wondering when I would see the summit flag. Each time I achieved one little hill, another would rise up behind it.

I became aware that one of the guides was shadowing me. When I moved, he moved. When I stopped, he stopped. Fifty paces, stop and rest. Fifty paces, stop and rest. Dawn came. The eastern sky lightened and revealed a giant abstract of lava and snow hundreds of feet below me on the crater's floor. To my left, as far as I could see, dropping off into forever, lay the snowfields of Kilimanjaro. As the sun rose, it bathed the world in a rosy-golden glow. The snow turned pink. The air turned pink, and the entire eastern sky flushed with the coming day. I stopped and savored the magnificence and then moved on. Fifty paces, stop and rest. Fifty paces, stop and rest.

Suddenly, I became aware of an arm around my waist as the guide linked himself to my quest for the summit. We moved in unison, fifty paces, stop and rest, fifty paces, stop and rest. At one point, I turned slightly and asked, "What is your name?" "William," came the soft reply. Fifty paces, stop and rest.

At last I mounted the hillock which granted me the view I had been seeking so long, the green and yellow flag that marks Uhuru, a word that in Swahili means "peace." Uhuru, at 19,360 feet, is the summit of Mt. Kilimanjaro. With one last push of will, mind, body, muscle, and spirit, I propelled myself up over the slope and stood on the summit of Mt. Kilimanjaro.

William and I looked at each other for the first time as we wrapped each other in a giant hug, eyes dancing, grins flashing from ear to ear. It was a moment of pure celebration. It was a moment of pure, ecstatic human connection. There were no barriers between us, just joy, celebration, and mutual respect.

William and I surmounted vast differences to share in that glorious celebration atop Kilimanjaro. He was black, I was white. He was male, I was female. He was poor, I was rich. He was uneducated, I was educated. He was young, I was older. He spoke Swahili, I spoke English. And in those crystalline moments on the top of Mt. Kilimanjaro, none of those barriers existed.

LIVES OF DISCONNECTION

Consciousness is the hallmark of humanity. It is our consciousness that distinguishes us from the other animals of our planet. Consciousness is both blessing and curse. We understand that we have a free will and can choose to build our lives based on ideas and premises that are freely chosen. That is our greatest blessing. Simultaneously, our consciousness makes us responsible for the quality of our lives. Far too many of us perceive that as a curse and choose to live lives that are less satisfying, less fulfilling, less productive, and less joyful than they might be.

People today are disconnected. In fact the major dis-ease of our time is disconnection. We are disconnected from ourselves, from our hopes and dreams, and from each other. We are disconnected racially and ethnically and increasingly disconnected economically. We are disconnected from the reality that there really aren't any differences between us at all. Our humanity connects all to the other, and we live in denial of our commonality. The divisions we create, using categories that only a being of human intelligence could make up, so disconnect us that we are all too willing to rape, kill, and pillage because the "other" is known by a different name.

DISCONNECTED FROM WORK AND LOVE

All too many of us are disconnected from our work and simply do tasks that provide a modicum of living-expense money but do not satisfy the needs of our souls. Our work lives are disconnected from our "real lives." Our "real lives" are often so frantic and rushed that we are disconnected from our families by overheated schedules and lack of attention. When Freud talked about the human need "to work and to love," he wasn't referring to the frantic pace and unending demands that comprise so many contemporary jobs. Nor was he referring to the jobs of endless, mindless repetition that sap energy, initiative, and spirit. He was talking about engaging in productive activities that are a meaningful expression of self.

During the recession of the early nineties, I occasionally gave speeches to a job-networking support group in my area. During the depth of the recession the group attracted 200 - 250 people each week. When I spoke I would ask how many people really loved the jobs they had lost. Usually 25 - 30 people would raise their hands. When I asked how many of those people loved their jobs so much they would do them even if they didn't get paid, the hands would lower until only two or three were left. My instruction to those people whose hands were still up was that they should go out and do anything they could to recreate the jobs they had lost. All the rest of the people in the room were advised to stop looking for a job and start looking for the work that they loved so much they would do it even if they didn't get paid for it.

Americans live separated from the communities of the past, where neighbors knew, loved, and supported each other through good times and bad. I recently spoke with an American woman who is currently raising two young daughters. The family is living in Heidelberg, Germany. She commented about how much easier and more relaxed she is in Germany, knowing that there is a community in her neighborhood who watches out for her children even as she watches out for theirs.

A few years ago I spent three days sailing on the Nile River in a felluca. On the last scheduled day of sailing, we were forced off the river by high winds and spent the day tied to the shore. Three of the men in the group left the boat to go exploring in a nearby village. They encountered a young man who was on leave from the Egyptian Army. He invited them into his home where they were warmly welcomed and invited in to tea. When I heard the story, I could not help reflecting on the uneasiness I sometimes feel when someone comes to my door seeking help. There was no such hesitation or uneasiness on the part of that Egyptian family. Their sense of connection and community extended to strangers from other parts of the world.

People used to find a sense of community in their places of work. The destabilization of the workforce, the re-engineering, re-structuring, downsizing, rightsizing, and capsizing of the workplace has destroyed that arena of continuity and community. People can no longer invest in long-term friendships with the people with whom they work. They'll be working with different people tomorrow and forging connections with new people rather than deepening connections with those they already call "friend."

Americans have less leisure time than they did a generation ago. We are working longer hours with less satisfaction. Many families are three and four-job families, leaving little time or energy for anything else in their lives except work. In spite of a booming economy, people are fearful of losing their jobs. Few people are passionately and creatively connected to work that they love or communities where they experience connection, support, and continuity.

DISCONNECTED FROM REALITY

We spend many hours in front of the television disconnected from reality, vicariously experiencing programs that too many of us substitute for real life. The average American spends 25 hours per week watching television, one full day each week spent in a pseudo-life. Watching actors and actresses portray made-up characters acting in made-up scenes is hardly living. When my children were little, we referred to watching television as "numbing out." As they settled in to watch television, they descended into a semi-stuporous state where they were oblivious to the world around them—and to the world inside them.

Others of us disconnect from reality with drugs—street or prescription, alcohol, or nicotine. A recent newspaper article reported that there are 28 million people using Prozac in this country. We're even getting Prozac prescriptions for our dogs! More and more children are being placed on antidepressants and other medications to control their moods and behaviors. In addition to Prozac there are other serotonin uptake inhibitors that we're gobbling like candy. Television commercials push drugs with more vigor that any street drug merchant. For whatever human ailment, physical or emotional, the "American way" seems to be medicate it. The medicines don't usually fix the problems. They just create a chemical barrier between us and the problems, disconnecting us. The side effect of the drugs is that we are subtly learning that we lack the resources to solve our problems. We train ourselves to be passive. We learn to seek relief rather than to seek solutions.

We live in a society that long ago declared a "war on drugs." We have thrown billions of dollars at the problem while drug usage has gone on unabated. According to the U.S. Department of Health and Human Services' *Preliminary Estimates from the 1995 National Household Survey on Drug Abuse*, almost thirteen million people over the age of 12 admitted to illicit drug use in 1995. The rate of drug use among youth has doubled since 1992. Heroin use and marijuana use are both on the rise. One quarter of us still use cigarettes, partially for the mind-altering effects of the nicotine, and we smoke with full knowledge of the dangers of cigarettes. Alcohol is one of the more popular drugs, so common that most people do not even consider alcohol a drug. Alcohol abuse costs American business $100 billion dollars per year according to a Robert Wood Johnson study reported in *Healthy, Wealthy & Wise: Fundamentals of Workplace Health Promotion* by the Wellness Councils of America. The same study reports that health insurance claims are twice as high for employees who drink and that 40 percent of hospitalized patients are admitted because of illnesses related to alcoholism. Twenty-one percent of the population over the age of twelve reports either heavy drinking (more than two drinks per day) or binge drinking. Far too many of us treat alcohol as a harmless social ritual—and maybe for some it is. For others it is a deadly drug. For all who use it, it is a mechanism of disconnection, disconnection from feeling anxious or tense, disconnection from boredom, or disconnection from realities of life that are unbearable.

Americans take drugs as easily as they breathe. We use caffeine to wake up and sedatives to go to sleep. We gobble up diet pills so we can continue to gobble down food. We rush to the medicine chest to "relieve minor aches." If they are "minor," why do they need treatment at all? We even use drugs to move our bowels. I'm not arguing that there is no place for drugs in the treatment of illness. Thank goodness we have the amazing capacity to treat the illnesses we do with effective drugs. Drugs certainly do much to relieve human suffering. But we rely too heavily on them and too often use them as a vehicle to disconnect from our problems.

All of the drugs we use for altering our minds are a form of "numbing out." We take them to feel better, but our use of them guarantees that we will stay disconnected from our real feelings and experiences. Psychological pain is a powerful motivator to make changes in our lives. By treating the symptoms, we improve how we feel and continue to ignore the underlying cause. It is only in treating the underlying causes that we can change our lives. It is only in treating the underlying causes that we can move from a life of "quiet desperation" to one of freedom, growth, and joy.

DISCONNECTED FROM MASCULINITY/FEMININITY

Although women have made great strides in the last two decades too many of us are still disconnected from the masculine aspects of our personalities. We live disconnected from great pieces of our potential. In *Women Who Run With the Wolves*, Dr. Clarissa Pinkola Estés says that all women at some point in middle age make a decision about whether they are going to be bitter old women. The etiology of the bitterness is the growing knowledge of a life not fully lived, of discovering the level of disconnectedness from true self that has been accepted.

The devaluing of the "feminine" attributes separates women from being connected to the totality of their beauty and strength. The richness and value of women's proclivity for emotion and relationships has been seen as having less value than the traditional masculine strengths of linear thought and taking action. I was once passed over for a promotion in a work setting where people were very unhappy and stressed because I was a "facilitator." The real shame was not that my facilitation skills were seen as less valued than a more masculine aggressive approach, but that I came to the same conclusion. Instead of seeing the skills I brought as equally valuable, I internally agreed with the decision and devalued myself. In fact, a facilitative approach to the internal problems of the organization were exactly what was needed.

Far too many men have great difficulty in connecting with the feminine aspects of themselves. They live disconnected from their gentleness and affection, from their fears and vulnerabilities. One tragic fallout of the homophobia in this country is the pressure it puts on men to be "manly," i.e., unfeeling and remote. Young boys quickly learn from their peers that any displays of "softness" will get them labeled as "sissies" or "faggots." They quickly learn that to display feelings is to humiliate themselves, so the feelings go underground. The boy gets disconnected from a part of himself. Three or four decades later he finds himself in an unhappy marriage with his wife complaining that he doesn't share his feelings. The dis-connect from his feelings impedes his ability to connect with the closest people in his life—his most significant others.

As a result of the lack of balance between *animus* and *anima,* both sexes are disconnected from the potential of being fully human. The range of responses and skills that are possible for human beings is limited when people restrict themselves to roles based on gender lines. To be whole, to be healthy, both sexes need to be fully developed in both masculine and feminine skills, aptitudes, and attitudes.

At the moment, it seems easier for women to be connected to their masculine aspects than vice-versa. Men are lagging behind in their ability to break free of the cultural stereotypes and express their feelings, to touch except in the context of sex, or to show their concerns and vulnerabilities. It is almost as if men channel all their feelings into one narrow band of expression, a funnel with all the feelings going into the wide end and squeezing out the other as anger—all too often exploding out the other end as anger.

When my son Adam was born, I was determined to rear a son who was comfortable and conversant with his feelings. He was given permission to express his feelings, allowed to cry, and never was told to "act like a man." At age fifteen, he purchased a secondhand moped with his own money. He was so excited about his first pair of wheels, that symbol of adulthood and freedom. When he got the moped home, he discovered that he couldn't get it to start. No amount of cursing, swearing, or mechanical adjustment worked. He was furious. He ranted, he raved, he yelled. His stream of angry words hardly slowed as we got in the car to return the machine. The malfunction was fixed and the crisis was over.

Later I observed that I knew how distressed and disappointed he was. He responded, "Well, I did want to cry." And then I felt like crying. Somehow, in spite of my efforts to the contrary, Adam's range of emotion was constricted and narrowed. His birthright of a wide range of emotion was now buried beneath the cultural injunctions of manhood.

Men typically die ten years before women. This narrowing of emotion is as deadly as the constriction of coronary arteries. Heart disease is not just about cholesterol levels and plaque buildup. Men, disconnected from their emotions, are also prematurely disconnected from their lives. I speculate that when men are able to be more freely connected to their emotions this discrepancy in life expectancy will diminish.

Both men and women live disconnected from each other or yoked in mutual dependent anger. The ecstatic bonding between men and women is all too often a fleeting "falling in love" bonding which does not survive the daily-ness of life. During the exciting, expansive early stages of love, couples are open to, appreciative of, and delighted with, the totality of the other. As time goes on, the pattern of closing down to each other, being less interested, appreciative, and available, creates a gulf between the partners. They become less conscious of the other and all too often merely live side by side, going through life rather like small children engaging in parallel play in a sandbox, playing in the same arena, but not really connected, not really sharing in the intimacy that provides such pleasure and satisfaction. A primary significant relationship which should be a major connection to Self and with Self becomes an agent of loneliness.

DISCONNECTED FROM OUR ENVIRONMENT

We live and work inside heated, air conditioned buildings and drive air-conditioned cars. That keeps us disconnected from the natural world that our species has been intimately connected with for thousands of years. The noise of contemporary Western living keeps us from the silence and quiet spaces of the outdoors, which were so much more easily accessible to our forebears. We are segregated from the beauty of the sunrise and from awareness of the phases of the moon. We are too busy to notice the smell of earth in spring, the sounds of the brook as it lies chuckling in its bed, or the daily changes in the growth of the leaves on the trees in our yards. Many of us are so disconnected from the natural world that we do not even have trees in our yards. I believe that humans in developed societies have a hunger for the natural world and that our pleasure in living is diminished by our separation from the outdoors. When we are unconscious of our environment we live diminished lives. Wayne Dyer has a wonderfully expressive term when he calls humans, "environorganisms." Indeed, we are environorganisms but most of us live disconnected from that concept. Our lack of consciousness about our connection impoverishes our lives.

DISCONNECTED FROM OUR PHYSICALITY

Many of us are disconnected from our physical selves. We sit in front of the television hour after hour with too little energy to get up off the couch to change the channel, so we surf with the remote. We are so addicted to our labor-saving devices that we even use electric can openers, which seem to me to be one of the more ludicrous inventions ever sold to man—or woman. How much effort does it take to open a can of beans? We wage combat to get the parking place closest to the door or drive in circles around the mall looking for a place close to the door when there are dozens a few yards away that would require a three minute walk. We eat when we are not hungry or we starve ourselves in an effort to be thin. Some of us even resort to vomiting to get rid of the excess food we've consumed. We get too little sleep. We seem to be in denial about the importance of our physical well-being as it relates to the quality of our lives. We act as if our bodies can run along forever without ever getting tuned up. Most of us take better care of our cars than we do our bodies. People who wouldn't dream of skipping an oil change on the Buick are content to let their bodies deteriorate and decay.

Women, and increasingly men, are disconnected from valuing and appreciating their physical bodies. The standards of beauty are so distorted that few women are satisfied, or even delighted with, their physical selves. When I speak on fitness I usually challenge the audience to tell me five adjectives that describe the ideal female in this culture. I further challenge them to give me all five adjectives within thirty seconds. The adjectives are "tall, thin, tan, blonde, and young." No audience ever fails to come up with the adjectives and few miss the thirty second mark. I then spend time discussing the realities of any of us ever meeting the standard. The average woman is 5 feet, 4 inches tall. Models are close to six feet—right there most of us are eliminated from meeting the standard by our genetics. I can personally attest that no amount of eating right, exercising, or wanting to be taller will increase your height. The thin standard has become so thin that anorexic models "dis"grace the covers of our magazines and little girls all over the country sigh and "want to be just like her." We know that tanning causes skin cancer and wrinkles. Now that's certainly beautiful! Blonde is possible for all of us as long as Clairol and L'Oreal stay in business. Young is something that happens to us once. It doesn't last long and for most of us, it's done.

We make ourselves crazy trying to meet a standard that can never be met. In the process we direct loathing at ourselves, diminish our self-esteem, and live separated from our wonderful physicality. The standards for men are not as ridiculous as they are for women, but men are increasingly self-conscious and self-disparaging about their looks.

Being disconnected from our physicality keeps us separated from parts of ourselves. The word psychosomatic is interesting in this regard. Psychosomatic illness has been seen as less than legitimate. People suffering from psychosomatic illness get labeled as "cranks" and "crocks" and are seen as less deserving than those suffering from physical illness. How inaccurate that view is! And what a disservice it does to the integrity of our human experience. Psyche and soma do not snap apart like Legos. What happens in your mind happens in your body and vice-versa. If you doubt this, go to a horror movie or an erotic film and monitor your body for signs of physiological response. I guarantee you'll find it. The very fact that we respond physically to what we are watching is a basic reason why we attend such movies. We want the physical response. Experiencing the connection of our minds and bodies in a darkened movie theater makes us feel alive!

Some Asian languages recognize the inherent unity of the physical and mental aspects of humanity. They have one word which means heart and mind. In the West for hundreds of years we have segregated and separated parts of ourselves so effectively that our language is devoid of a unified term. In order for me to communicate the concept, I have to write "mind/body."

Our language however, is laced with sayings that recognize the inherent truth of the integrity of our physical and mental selves (even separating mind and body in this sentence is reducing our experience to less than the sum of its parts). We speak of being "sick at heart," or of someone as being a "pain in the neck." Although our language recognizes the integrity of the connection of physical and mental, we all too often live as if there were no connection, just as there is no single word.

If I could separate the ingredients of a cake into its parts, removing the sugar and the flour and the vanilla, I would no longer have a cake. I would simply have the ingredients for the cake. I would be left with something less than the whole. In the same way when I separate my body from my mind, I am rendering myself less than whole, less than the total expression of who I am.

As our scientific capacity increases we are seeing more and more research evidence that there is no separation of mind and body. Cells all over our bodies have neuroreceptor sites, docking places for the chemicals that we once thought were only found in brain tissue. Work by Herbert Benson, Joan Boryshenko, and Jon Kabat-Zinn represent a major reconnection for our thinking. Serious academic work is helping people understand the integrity of their mind/bodies.

The socialization we underwent as children laid the groundwork for the alienation from our physical selves. We were told not to run when we wanted to run, to eat when we were not hungry, and to wait until dinner when we were hungry. And some of us at the table were told how much of just what we could eat, regardless of what our own internal signals were telling us. We were told when to go to sleep. We learned that we should not pick our noses or scratch certain parts of our bodies (it seems that only major league ball players are allowed latitude here). We were told to sit still when every cell in our bodies longed to move.

Many of us eat to manage feelings. We use the food to assuage the emotions which often we don't stop to identify or reckon with. As a result we are disconnected from the feelings and from the processes of our bodies that govern our hunger and appetite.

We are disconnected from each other physically as well. Touch is highly regulated and controlled. We learn early in life to be restrained and reserved in how we touch others. Although there are cultural differences, far too many of us are constrained by the cultural norms about touching. Babies who are not held and cuddled exhibit "failure to thrive" syndrome. Some even die. It doesn't seem logical that a species that depends on touching as a major ingredient of nurturing its young would suddenly stop wanting to touch and be touched when maturity is reached. The fact is we are touch deprived and touch-hungry.

Women have more latitude in touching than men do. Women have a cultural advantage in the more permissive attitude toward our use of touch. Male touching is more limited, mostly focused around sex. Homophobia and tradition usually limit male touching to handshakes, occasional hugs, and pats on the fanny during athletic contests. Touching is a marvelous way of soothing one another as well as expressing care, concern, and love. It is a loss to our well-being to have its expression so limited.

One of the off-shoots of our awareness of the prevalence and ugliness of sexual abuse is that to protect ourselves from abuse we are further limiting the amount of touching. In my career as a psychiatric nurse, I grew to be concerned about how I used touch to comfort patients who were suffering enormous emotional pain. It deeply bothered me when I had to evaluate the decision of whether to reach out and hug someone. I wondered whether it would be considered abusive, particularly when I knew how deeply in need of being hugged the person was.

DISCONNECTED FROM PLAYING

We are cut off from our playful selves. Did you ever wonder why adults let children get away with being the only ones to play? If adults control the world, why are children the only ones who play? Play, as used by children, is a means of learning, an avenue of connection with peers, and a way of energizing and revitalizing. Play is just as useful for adults for the same reasons. It is sad that we are disconnected from our playfulness and, thus, our creativity. The spontaneous creative play of childhood is being replaced by regimented activities. Our children's lives are becoming as overcommitted as adults' lives as they rush from school to sports to music lessons to homework to bed. Then they get up the next morning to repeat the cycle, dashing madly along the road to "success." The pressure to be "doing" extracts a great price from our children's "being." It is out of our "being" that spontaneous creativity and play arises. It's no wonder that our children are being given Prozac along with our dogs.

It is a rare person who does not respond with warmth and enthusiasm to small children playing and laughing with freedom and delight. We usually respond in the same way to puppies or kittens gamboling. I think it is the recognition of lost parts of ourselves that elicits the response. In their play we see ourselves. In their play we recognize the elemental connection to Life, the generative, creative, powerful flow of life that we all share. Too many of us settle for a vicarious experience of playfulness rather than creating it for ourselves. The Talmud reminds us, in the world to come each of us will be called to account for all the good things God put on this earth that we refused to enjoy.

THE DISCONNECT OF DENIAL

Most of us spend far too much of our lives disconnected from ourselves through the mechanism of denial. We deny our true feelings, our hurts, our pains, our fears, and our hopes. Even worse, we deny our potential for achievement, for mastery, and for greatness. We deny the past events of our lives, our histories, and in so doing, disconnect ourselves from our present and our presence. Denial keeps us absent from our own lives, rendering us mere shadows of our present and potential selves.

Far too many of us are disconnected from our consciousness, the consciousness that distinguishes us from other mammals and which distinguishes the living from the dead. The more conscious one is the more alive one is. Far too many of us are moving physically about the face of the earth, performing tasks, doing things, but only as dead people masquerading as the living. Too many of us live lives in shades of black and white and gray. To make the decision to live as fully consciously as possible is to change the film and live life in full technicolor.

Another area of disconnectedness is from our spectacular uniqueness. There has never been anyone just like you nor will there ever be. No one ever had the unique combination of qualities and potentials that you do. If you don't develop your potentials to the highest degree that you can, they will forever go unrealized. Far too few people ever explore the parameters of themselves, defining and expressing their potential, seeking and developing the expression of themselves. For one thing, it requires work, self-discipline, determination, and courage. We live in a time when we seem to want it to be easy. We are used to quick results, not stopping to consider that the realization of a spectacular life takes time and the ability to withstand pressure, just as the realization of a diamond requires time and pressure.

Many of us bear deep burdens of shame and tell ourselves that we are "not good enough" to be all that we might be. We get told in many large and small ways that we do not have "what it takes." We hear that we are "shy," or "slow," or "not artistic," or "not as good an athlete" as our brother was. We learn that "pride goeth before a fall." We learn that it is better to be safe than sorry and that we'd better give up the big dreams because the odds against our succeeding are so high. And after hearing the message too many times we give up our dreams and settle for the level that we think we can achieve. We forget what we once knew as children, that life is good, that we are good, and that we are supposed to enjoy this experience, to use it as a source of learning and joy. We forget that we can be really connected to ourselves and also to others. We are so dis-couraged, literally separated from our hearts, that we no longer attempt to live the hero's life that is the full possibility for any of us. We doubt our validity and live in the shadows.

Far too many of us decide what we can have and then decide what we want. We should decide what we want and then learn just how much we can have. This book is written for those of you who want to live more fully than you are now, for those of you who sense that something is missing and you want more. It is for those of you who understand that more limits have been placed on you than are healthy for you. It is for those of you who want to live, fully, richly, deeply.

For many years I have commented that life is a smorgasbord and that I intend to sample as much as I possibly can while I live. Only recently did I learn that Mame (of *Auntie Mame* fame) uttered the smorgasbord comparison, and I had unknowingly plagiarized it for many years. Thanks Mame, it's a great line and a great philosophy. To life! To connection and health and wholeness.

Action Steps

1. Start a "dream journal." In it write down things that you would like to have or do or be in your life. Do not censor what your write by critiquing whether it's possible or not. If it is something that you would like to have write it down.
2. On paper write your responses to the following sentence stems:
   - If I were more connected to my Self, I would...
   - If I were more connected to my physicality, I would...
   - If I expressed the masculine aspects of myself more freely, I would...
   - If I expressed the feminine aspects of myself more freely, I would...
   - Things in my life which obstruct my happiness are...
   - Some of the things that I would do if I had the time are...
   - If I learned today that I had six months left to live, I would like to do...
   - I am happiest when...
   - I am saddest when...
   - If I died tomorrow, I would regret...
3. Think of someone from whom you feel disconnected. Write them a letter in which you talk about the good things that the two of you have

shared and what you regret about the disruption in your relationship. Decide if you want to mail the letter.
4. Make a list of the times when you have experienced the ecstasy of totally open connection with other humans. When you are feeling lonely or disconnected, re-read what you have written and use the information as a road map to build more of those connections in your life.

Points to Ponder
- Your vision is your "I-sight."
- Relationships, like investments, either appreciate or depreciate. To compound your returns, appreciate those you love, frequently and often.
- How you view the future determines how you live today. How you live today determines your future.
- Isn't it interesting that most people want to make progress and simultaneously resist change?
- Did you ever notice that frequently people treat total strangers with more courtesy than they do family members?

Chapter 2

WHAT YOU KNEW WHEN YOU WERE TWO: UNCOVERING, RECOVERING, OR DISCOVERING SELF

WHEN I WAS TWO, my mother observed me crying one afternoon and commented to my Aunt Barbara, "When Rita cries she surely cries with enthusiasm." Barbara replied, "Whatever Rita does, she does with enthusiasm!"

I was eighteen and fat. All my life I had endured the taunts of friends, peers, and even a few adults. The school bus driver had kiddingly called me "Crisco—fat in the can." An older brother had berated and teased me mercilessly from my very early years. I didn't think I was smart enough to do college work, and when Mrs. Young, my English teacher told me during my senior year in high school that I should go to college, I shrugged her off saying that I wanted to be a nurse and nursing school would suffice for that. She replied that I should go to college. Shame prevented me from telling her the real reason I wasn't planning to attend college. I had reasoned it was better to set my sights low than to attempt and fail.

Another reason for not going to college was my family's lack of financial resources. I grew up on the coast of Maine as one of a family of nine children. During my childhood coastal Maine was an economically depressed area that offered few opportunities for my father who had given up his dreams of a college education to help support his family of origin during the Depression. During one awful winter when I was ten my father was out of work. I worried that the state would separate our family by placing us children in foster homes because of our economic situation. Of course, I could not discuss this with anyone, and bore the fear and humiliation alone.

High school had been fun for me. I did reasonably well academically and loved playing sports. Gym was my favorite subject. I was always puzzled by my classmates who seemed to have three or four periods per month so they could evade class. I thought running and jumping and yelling was a fine way to pass a 45 minute period.

But high school was also a time of humiliation for me. I didn't have the "right" clothes. My breasts weren't perky and pointed the way Barbara Jones' were. It never occurred to me that I might be attractive or even could be. Beauty was something that other girls had, not Rita Hennessey. I didn't have a boyfriend, and I never got asked out for a date. The boys would play one-on-one basketball with me but no one asked me to the prom. At that time, being part of a couple seemed to me to be "the" definition of success as a woman. I knew at a very deep level that I was a failure.

My parents were not bad parents. I knew I was deeply loved. I can remember thinking as an adolescent that there was nothing that I could ever do, even getting pregnant (as you know that was hardly a possibility!), that would make my parents stop loving me. But they were overwhelmed by their economics and large family. They didn't have the time or the awareness to see my struggles with a self-esteem that had shriveled as I had matured. And if they had seen it, I don't know that they would have known how to help me. My shame would have prevented me from acknowledging just how little regard I had for myself.

And so at eighteen, I left home to attend nursing school. I had no idea how bright I really was. I had no idea that I had real talent as an athlete. I didn't realize that I was a beautiful young woman. I carried around a collection of "self-inflicted" wounds.

If anyone had peered into the future and told me that I would be as I am today, writing my second book, supporting myself as a speaker, the owner of a doctorate, a one-time ultra distance triathlon national champion, a finisher of the Hawaii Ironman Triathlon, and a climber of Mt. Kilimanjaro, I would have told them they were nuts—totally, completely nuts. My self-esteem of that day could not have considered that I would do any of those things.

"SELF-INFLICTED" WOUNDS

I moved from the howlingly enthusiastic two-year old to the self-diminishing eighteen-year old as the result of "self-inflicted" wounds—

wounds to the Self. The effects of multiple assaults on my personal integrity, the labeling and stereo-typing of the "fat kid" who also wet her bed long past early childhood, the pressures to conform to the limited expectations of my gender, all created wounds on my "Self." I had more self-respect as that howling two-year old than I did as a high school graduate.

Each one of us is a unique, singular human being. There has never been anyone just like you in the entire history of the human race—and there never will be. Think of the implications of that. You are unique, special in ways that no one else ever has been. Isn't that miraculous? The design of the Universe is such that no one ever is a duplicate.

Each of us is designed to be an individual expression of Life. Your uniqueness means that no one else can be an authority on your life. No one else gets to live your experience, no one else should get to direct the terms on which you live your life. You can only live your *best* life if you are living the fullest expression of your *Self*.

No one escapes from childhood without some degree of "self-inflicted" wounds, those wounds to our sense of self that make it so difficult to live our own lives and follow our own paths. Even those of us who grew up in homes with very loving, well-intentioned parenting do not escape from the "self-erosion" of peers, teachers, coaches, religious leaders, or relatives. These wounds leave deep scars on our individuality and constrict the expression of self. Society, churches, schools, and other institutions are more interested in keeping the institutions intact than they are in allowing the freedom of self. At some level, all institutions fear self-expression based on the misperception that if we all lived fully as ourselves, anarchy would reign and society would descend into chaos. Individuals with high self-esteem, secure in the knowledge that they can get their needs met without inflicting harm on others, are the only real defense against chaos. The higher our self-esteem the more capable we are of living in peace and cooperating together for the greater good of the community. The higher a person's self-esteem the less the need to dominate others to feel important or powerful.

Too often, the process of socialization reduces self-esteem and disconnects us from the awareness of our uniqueness and our inherent value. We don't learn to respect our own judgment about how we should live our lives. Our experiences as children leave us as adults living life according to someone else's premises and rules. We trim off the edges of our uniqueness to make ourselves fit the societally prescribed mold. We wouldn't think of going through life in shoes that didn't quite fit, but too many of us go through life living by rules that don't quite fit. Shoes that don't fit leave blisters on our *soles*. Living by rules and premises that don't quite fit leave blisters on our *souls*.

The child who says he wants to be a writer and is met with a response of, "How will you make a living? Only a very few people ever make it as writers," is receiving a "self-inflicted" wound. The child who is told that she is stupid is receiving "self-inflicted" wounds. The child who says she wants to be an "astronaut and a policewoman and a writer and a musician" and is told that she can't be all of them, she must choose, is receiving a "self-inflicted" wound. The child who is labeled, "slow," "shy," "bully," or "nerd" is being wounded. All children who are abused in any way are also receiving "self-inflicted" wounds.

The really insidious power of "self-inflicted" wounds is that after a while, we incorporate the self-limiting, self-denigrating beliefs into ourselves. The wounds then become truly "self-inflicted." If you tie a baby elephant with a rope that he cannot break, you can keep him tied with a string when he is an adult. You create the belief in the baby that something tied around his leg means he is confined. When he is an adult a string will keep him confined. Our self-limiting beliefs, arising from "self-inflicted" wounds, also keep us confined. They limit our ability to create the fullest expression of our unique selves.

When I was a kid I learned the "self" defensive ditty, "Sticks and stones can break my bones, but names will never hurt me." I now know that those "names" inflicted more damage than physical injury. Physical tissue seems to have more healing capacity than psychic tissue. Or perhaps it's that parents and other adults immediately recognize the need to clean and dress a bleeding wound but are not as skilled at recognizing and treating the wounds of the spirit.

WHEN YOU WERE TWO

As two-year olds with budding personalities and a growing concept of self, we were quite connected to ourselves. We were learning how to differentiate ourselves from others. We were recognizing that what we wanted and what others wanted were not necessarily the same. Although my mother doesn't recall the incident that sparked my howling, it's highly likely that I wanted one thing and she wanted another. My howling represented my protest at a block to my self-determination. Although I couldn't articulate it, I understood that my Self was being thwarted and frustrated. At two, I hadn't been socialized enough to be polite or self-sacrificing, so I just howled in protest.

As two-year olds we were learning about our Selves and making a real issue of getting what we wanted, when we wanted it. As we entered the infamous "no" stage, we were asserting our right to be ourSelves, capable of expressing our wants and making demands of the world around us. When people around us started restricting our freedom and our expression, we roared back, "No!" We were defending against "self-inflicted" wounds. They were bigger and more powerful than we were, we were completely dependent on them for survival, and we wanted their approval because approval felt *so good*, so we learned to put their wants ahead of our own need for self-expression.

CONNECTED TO PHYSICALITY

As two-year olds, we were completely at home in, and at ease with our bodies. We didn't look in the mirror and say, "I hate my thighs," or "You are disgustingly fat," or "You are ugly." We looked into mirrors and were delighted with what we saw. We played with the image grinning back at us. We hadn't yet learned to compare ourselves to others and invariably see ourselves as lacking in some way. We also hadn't learned to look at others and judge them saying, "This one is much better looking than I," and "That one is so ugly." We just accepted ourselves and others as looking the way we looked.

We didn't have any compunction about being nude, sometimes to our parent's chagrin and dismay. We were fascinated with our bodies and the bodies of others. We brought the same childish curiosity to our bodies as we did to everything else we were discovering in the world. We were proud of our waste products and our ability to produce them. We knew that our bodies were good and we didn't feel ashamed of them. We freely experienced ourselves as physical beings. The integrity of our connections of body and mind hadn't yet been broken.

At the health club where I work out I am constantly reminded of how totally we've been separated from the integrity of body/mind and physical self. Most of the women who dress and undress in the locker room do so furtively. They duck into changing rooms or do elaborate dances with towels as they struggle to put damp skin into pantyhose without exposing any bare flesh. They are so thoroughly shamed by their physicality that they go to great lengths to hide from the scrutiny of other women. In a locker room for crying out loud!

Once in a while I see another woman who, like me, walks about comfortably nude. It makes me want to shout and cheer because I know I've encountered a sister who is refusing to allow "them" to make her feel ashamed of her body. I also recognize that she is likely making a statement about having broken free of some of the constraints imposed upon her. She has had the courage to confront the issue of shame about her physicality and move beyond it. The comfortable nude women in the locker room are making statements about their Selves and the integrity of their connection to their bodies.

Robert Karen writing in an *Atlantic Monthly* article entitled *Shame* (published in the February 1992 issue) discusses the process by which we deaden ourselves with shame. Some levels of shame, he says, are okay for us to acknowledge to ourselves but others are so humiliating that we refuse to admit them to consciousness. Those shames "dictate that the feared 'truth,' those ugly self-portraits, must never become conscious. Otherwise he will drown in self-hatred and lose the love, respect, and acceptance of even those closest to him. Hidden like this, shame can stalk one's being, inflicting an unconscious self-loathing."

Since our physical Self does not snap apart from our psychological/mental Self, we cannot be ashamed of our bodies without being ashamed of ourSelves. Being ashamed of ourselves is self-annihilation, a very debilitating state which cripples and deadens us.

As two-year olds we were in tune with, and connected to, and delighted in, our bodies. We tried to follow the dictates of our bodies and respond to the signals we received from them (which is really receiving signals from ourSelves). Left to our own devices, we ate what we wanted to eat when we were hungry. We ran and climbed when we wanted to run and climb. We stopped and rested when our bodies signaled that we needed to rest. Many of our "no-storms" were struggles with our parents to preserve the right to listen and respond to the dictates of our bodies.

As adults too many of us are totally cut off from the messages from our bodies. We have lost touch with, or only have tenuous connections to, our physical Selves. Our physical Selves are an essential component of our human experience. When our bodies are completely severed from our spirits, we are out of this life, dead. When we are only tenuously connected to our bodies, we are partially dead. We live lives that are less fulfilling and satisfying than they could be.

I sometimes comment that many of us are so totally cut off from our bodies that if we have any kind of sensation on the front of our bodies from the tops of our legs to the tip of our noses, we label it hunger and feed it. We are so disconnected from our physical Selves that we are unable to receive or decode bodily messages. No wonder one third of us are medically obese! Part of the knowledge that we had as two-year olds was in the pleasure of moving, climbing, running, and dancing. As adults a huge number of us think we've moved excessively when the remote is missing and we have to get up off the couch to change the channel!

Another whole aspect of our physicality that we learned to separate from as children was that of our sexuality. As two-year olds we knew that there were certain areas of our bodies that we could touch and experience as very pleasurable. We were quickly taught, verbally and nonverbally, that we shouldn't do that. We learned that parts of our bodies (read, parts of ourSelves) were dirty and not good. We learned to feel guilty about our sexual feelings. To deal with the discomfort of those feelings we drove them underground, into the unconscious, and disconnected with a vital part of ourselves. Certainly, we are not as sexually repressed as a culture as we were a few decades ago, but we're not completely comfortable and easy with it either. A recent conversation with a woman in her twenties astonished me. We were discussing our childhood education about sex. Her mother in the eighties avoided the whole topic, just as my mother did in the fifties, thirty years and a sexual revolution ago.

We had the ability to read those bodily signals when we were two, and we've lost it. The fear and shame that keep us from acknowledging the beauty of our bodies and sexuality is grounded in fear—fear that we will be found wanting by others, and fear that if we acknowledge the feelings we will lose control of our behavior. The truth is the more freely we allow ourselves to experience our feelings, the freer we are to consciously choose our actions. It is repressed feelings that cause us to lose control, not acknowledged, accepted feelings.

PERSISTENCE

When we were two we were persistent, again often to our parent's chagrin and frustration. Because our desire to have what we wanted conflicted with what our parents wanted, we got pressured or punished until we complied. Then, years later we take assertiveness training classes to re-learn what we knew when we were two. Granted, we lacked finesse, skill, and the consideration of other's needs in the expression of our self-assertion as two-year olds, but we had the basic concept.

When my younger son, Alden, was small, he was exceptionally persistent in getting what he wanted. One day I found myself commenting about how stubborn he was. Stubborn is a negative slant on persistence. On questioning myself about the labeling I was doing, I discovered that the quality he was displaying was being seen as stubborn only because he was a child. When he was an adult, those same behaviors would be labeled as persistent and held in positive light. I recognized that what I needed to do was help him learn to be more socially skilled in his assertion but that I certainly did not want him to lose the ability to persist. Persistence is, after all, a hallmark of heroism.

As children we all knew that the way to get something you wanted was to keep going after it. As a child my Uncle John told his older siblings about something he wanted to do. They counseled him that their father would say no. He then said he was going to ask his mother. They assured him that he would get a "no" there as well. He then said that he would ask the grandmother who lived with the family. They asked, "When Ganna says no, what are you going to do?" His reply: "Then I'll ask her a hundred times."

Some of us are so disconnected from what we want and its legitimacy that we don't even ask once, let alone persist a hundred times. The reality is that in order to get what we want sometimes we have to ask a hundred times. I am reminded of an old joke about the woman who was being shown around heaven by God. God had told her that she could see everything. They walked through the most magnificent opulence the woman had ever seen. God was happily showing her the delights of heaven when they came to a door that She didn't unlock. "Wait," the woman told God, "You told me I could see everything." God said, "Well that's true, but I don't think you really want to look in there." "Oh, yes," said the woman, "I most certainly do." God opened the door and they entered a huge room full of luxury cars. The woman wandered among the cars, oohing and aahing. Then she noticed that the cars all had name tags on them. She stopped dead in her tracks (pun intended!) and said, "God, this Rolls has my name on it! Why didn't I ever get it?" God sadly replied, "You always asked for a Ford."

As adults we tend to be disconnected from our ability to persist when the world is saying "No" to us. We attempt something and don't get the result we want, and because we've lost our connection to our persistence, we simply give up. Instead of going back, perhaps re-working our plan, and asking again, we give up on the dream or the goal. And when we give up on dreams and goals, we are goring ourselves with "self-inflicted" wounds.

COMFORTABLE WITH SAYING, "I DON'T KNOW."

As two-year olds we were insatiably curious about and delighted in the world which was unfolding around us. That world is still unfolding all around us and we are oblivious to it for the most part. As two-year olds, we could take great delight in fuzzy brown caterpillars or wriggling earthworms. We were fascinated by the stars above us and the dust bunnies under our beds. We wanted to know how things worked, what they were for, and what other ideas we could come up with for them. We were hungry little learning machines. We weren't bored by, or turned off by, anything. We just wanted to know. Later, as three-year olds we moved into the "why" stage where our search for knowledge took us beyond our parents' understanding and patience as we repeated, "Why? Why? Why?"

As a by-product of our socialization and experiences, most of us have shut down great parts of that life-giving wish to learn and to know. The free-ranging learning machines that we were as two-year olds quickly learned to "color within the lines" and to compare ourselves with others. We weren't rewarded for originality and creativity as often as we were for producing ideas and products that conformed to the teacher's expectations.

The world we live in today demands constant learning. Because we are historically at a junction where knowledge is exploding, everyone needs to be a learning machine. Technology has created a world where on-going learning at a rapid pace is necessary to be functional. Learning is essential to living a good life. Never have the opportunities for and the need for creativity been higher. We need to re-connect with our two-year old delight in learning.

Two-year olds don't worry about asking "stupid" questions. They are uninhibited in their willingness to ask when they are curious about something. Too often as adults, we hesitate to ask about something for fear that people will think we're stupid. An opportunity to expand our knowledge passes by.

When I was in my early thirties, I found myself curious about my reluctance to ask about things that I didn't know and realized it was because I didn't want to expose my ignorance and be judged as lacking (a place of vulnerability for a woman who already questioned her intellectual capacity). As I thought about it, I realized that there was no possible way for me to know everything. Therefore, it was not a matter of shame that I didn't know something. Freed from the shame, I gave myself the permission I'd had as a two-year old, to ask if I wanted to know. What I have discovered is that most people are delighted to answer questions. If they're interested in something, they usually love sharing the information. My asking is usually interpreted as a gift to them, and my learning new things is certainly a gift to myself.

Two-year olds are usually okay about a rapidly changing world. They aren't experienced enough to know how things "should" be, so when things are in flux and change they don't get anxious or upset about the loss of the "good old days." One of the most difficult things for humans to do is to unlearn old "truths." We simply are more comfortable with the old way. There is always a tug between growth and stability. As two-year olds, we weren't so invested in what *was* that we shut down to the possibilities of what *could be*.

As a result, we are adept at changing when we are two. The world we now live in requires that we adapt a two-year old's attitude toward change, which is "I'll flow with it. I'm ready to explore what's new." The future belongs to the flexible. Humans of the 21st century who cannot change and adapt rapidly are dinosaurs and dodos.

POSITIVE SELF-REGARD

If we were reared in a home where there was a measure of love, support, respect, and nurturance, as two-year olds we learned to like ourselves. We felt good about being alive and being who we were. In short, we were connected to the fledgling Self that we were in a positive way. Fledgling though it was, we had positive self-regard. A two-year old who has just built a towering structure of vegetable cans will bask in praise of her work. Indeed, she will even seek out the praise and verbalize her pride in her accomplishment and herSelf. My two-year old niece grinned at her mother one day as she exclaimed, "I's so cute!" What a shame to lose that self-appreciation.

A two-year old's self-pride is too often replaced by self-doubts and shame by the time he graduates from high school. When praised for graduating with high honors, lettering in several sports, getting accepted to nine prestigious colleges on full scholarship, he is all too apt to say, "It was nothing." He has been disconnected from the rightful pride of a job well-done. He has been disconnected from himSelf.

Two-year olds don't "should" on themselves. They don't berate themselves for real or imagined short-comings. They don't base their self-worth on how many things they've crossed off their "to-do" lists for the day. Children are willing to let the day unfold as it does. They have the freedom to live fully in each moment because they are not yet separated from themSelves. They haven't yet learned that they "should" be busy being human "doings." They are simply free to be growing, learning, human beings.

The socialization process separates us from basic self-sustaining efforts. We learn to submerge and stifle our own self-interest in the interest of approval from others. We are taught that it is good to be selfless and bad to be selfish. No one ever suggested that we should be "self-more." No one ever taught us that we could only diminish ourselves so many times before we disappeared.

Turned loose as two-year olds, none of us would survive. For all our integration and connection with our Self as two-year olds, we lacked knowledge, judgment, and self-discipline. We needed adult judgment and knowledge to keep us safe. Unfortunately, in the interest of physical and psychological safety, we learned to give away pieces of our Self, to submerge our true thoughts and feelings, to remain silent, to shade the truth, and deny our feelings in the process. The rebelliousness of adolescence is another attempt to reclaim and re-assert Self, but for most the ultimate choice is to conform and comply. Time quickly passes and another generation is living "lives of quiet desperation."

In order to live successfully, we need to combine the connection with community that is part of our innate need structure as human beings and the connection with Self that is the basis of our freedom and integrity. Living successfully also requires that we maintain the energetic, free-flowing connection with life that we knew as two-year olds and develop the adult capacities and strengths of judgment, knowledge, and self-discipline. The dynamic enthusiasm of a two-year old combined with the judgment, knowledge, and discipline of a thoughtful adult is the combination that creates real Self-power. That is the power that creates a unique life that brings value and benefit to all—to the person who is living it and all those that person interacts with.

When I did the *Artist's Way* (a wonderful course that everyone should complete whether they want to free their creativity and pursue their art or whether they just want to live more freely), one of our assignments was to write a lullaby. I wanted to sing to all the world's babies that they were beautiful, strong, lovable, and wonderful. As are you.

Sabrina's Song

You are so beautiful, you are so strong,
You are so wonderful, listen in your heart to the words of my song.

You are so beautiful, you are so free,
You are so wonderful, expression of Life in all that you'll be.

You are so beautiful, a child of great Grace,
You are so wonderful, dancing so lightly across time and space.

You are so beautiful, a gift of great Love,
You are so wonderful, a pleasure on earth from heav'n above.

You are so beautiful, you are so strong,
You are so wonderful, listen in your heart to the words of
your song.

You are so beautiful, you are so strong,
You are so wonderful, listen in your heart to the words of
your song.

Action Steps

1. Get out the old photo albums or movies shot when you were a two-year old. Look at the person you see in the pictures. What clues do you get about the core Self that you see in the pictures? Allow yourself to reconnect with the freedom and joy you felt at that age. If you don't have pictures, spend some time remembering or imagining what it was like to be two.
2. Spend some time with a two-year old. Most parents of a two-year old would be delighted to have an afternoon off while you spend time seeing the world from a two-year old's perspective. What attitudes or actions do you observe that might be useful for you to incorporate into your life?
3. Take a day for yourself to live like a two-year old. Eat what you want, when you want, explore everything, allow yourself to notice and be fascinated by the details of the world around you. If you want to be cuddled and held, ask someone to cuddle. You probably will decide that you don't want to do the temper tantrum in the supermarket bit, but if you want to run and climb trees or make sandcastles, do so. Whatever you do, don't mess the day up by telling yourself that you shouldn't be acting like a child—that's just the point. And don't feel guilty about goofing off. You are doing research!
4. Write down a list of topics that interest you. They don't need to have practical application or "value." Choose one topic, then go to the library and get a book or a tape on the subject or take a course.
5. Set learning goals each week. Have fun with your explorations.

Points to Ponder
- Kids who lose change the rules of the game.
- To be successful, keep the hope, energy, and enthusiasm of the beginning alive throughout the process, whether it is a job, a project—or your life.
- Self-esteem is built one risk, one change, one thought at a time.
- Change is the status quo. Losee, 1985
- Rapid change is the status quo. Losee, 1995

Chapter 3
MAKING FRIENDS WITH DISCIPLINE

THE OFFICE WHERE I SAT *was close and hot. I wasn't sure whether it was the room that was generating the heat or my own discomfort and tension. I was eighteen and had gone to Maine Medical Center where I was applying for entry into the School of Nursing. Mrs. Carolyn Jones was interviewing me. I felt so awkward and uncertain sitting across from this attractive, nicely dressed and well-groomed woman. I was acutely aware of the girdle and nylons that I had donned for the occasion. Rather than making me feel grown up and sophisticated, they made me feel like an imposter.*

Mrs. Jones was so nice that she relieved my tension somewhat as she gave me feedback on the psychological profile I had taken. I only remember one of my scores. I was totally dismayed when she reported I had scored in the 3rd percentile on persistence. That meant of 100 people taking the test, 97 scored higher than I on persistence. Mrs. Jones merely shrugged and said, "Sometimes these results come back crazy. Yours is one of those. I know that you are more persistent than the test shows. You've finished 3rd grade so you have to have more persistence than that."

She was right. I did have enough persistence to get through school. But I also think the test was quite accurate in picking up a weak area for me. I was great at starting something and not finishing it. For years afterwards, I would joke that if I were a musician I would be best known for my unfinished symphony.

I was undisciplined.

Years later, I was swimming in a national championship triathlon (a competitive event in which contestants swim over a course, then bicycle for a distance, and finish by running; distances vary). The swim distance in this race was one mile. I was a proficient swimmer and was usually very strong.

This race was not as comfortable for me as usual. It was a championship race so everyone was keyed up and tense. We were racing outside of Las Vegas in unusually cold weather. Before the race, I huddled, dressed in a full-body wetsuit, on the sunny side of the dumpster attempting to stay warm.

When my wave of racers went into the water, I was shocked by the cold even through my wetsuit. I ran into the water and started to swim. The water was so cold that I had difficulty breathing. All my body wanted to do was gasp. In addition, there was a current and choppy waves that kept splashing into my face, nose, and lungs when I tried to breathe. There were also other contestants, most of them bigger, more aggressive men, and I kept getting hit by elbows and feet.

I'd been through this kind of experience before, so I told myself just to settle down, to stay calm, that I was okay. I was saying the words with the rational part of my mind but the emotional part kept getting on top and telling me how scared and anxious I was. As I struggled toward the first turn, I battled with my anxiety and my emotion. I was not a happy racer.

Gradually, I became aware of a new thought. "You could quit." At first the words were quietly suggested against the background of my swirling emotion, but they kept getting louder and more distinct. Now instead of dismissing the concept, I was seriously considering it, weighing the pros and cons as I continued to swim, trying to find a rhythm and trying to find space without arms and legs, and trying to take air, not water, into my lungs.

The more I thought about quitting, the more appealing the idea became. About halfway to the buoy, I agreed with the voice urging me to quit. I decided to quit. I wasn't having any fun and that was my main goal for doing triathlons. The instant I made the quit decision, I heard from another part of myself. This little persona who looks and sounds just like me jumped out of my conscious and roared at me, "You will not quit! You just get to that turn-around buoy, and then you can decide if you want to quit or not. I don't care how you get there, you just get there any way you can, but you're not quitting now."

I was psyching myself, and I knew it. I knew that the current and the waves would be behind me once I made the turn. I knew that the crowd would thin out as well. So I flipped on my side and side-stroked most of the rest of the way to the buoy. It wasn't what I'd planned, but it got me to the turn. I finished the swim well and went on to have a good race—and a good time.

I had learned an invaluable skill. I had learned to be disciplined.

Self-discipline and self-reliance are not commodities that enjoy great popularity in the United States today. This country was settled by people who were willing to risk everything in order to gain freedom and opportunity. We have become a nation of whiners who want certainty and security. We want (no, demand) that all the danger be taken out of our lives. We expect someone else to take responsibility for us. There has been much media attention paid to health care over the past few years. The crux of the question is, "Who's going to pay for the treatment of disease?" I read or hear very little about our personal responsibility to take care of ourselves so that we don't become diseased in the first place.

It is insane for a health insurance company to pay $50,000 - $60,000 for coronary bypass surgery for a smoker who continues to smoke and then needs another surgery or angioplasty. Where's the individual's responsibility for having the self-discipline to take care of himself and quit smoking? It is equally insane for people to have 15 - 20 detoxifications for drug or alcohol abuse and expect society to keep right on picking up the tab.

Last summer I bought a step ladder. There were four separate stickers warning users in the safe use of the ladder. It is obvious that the stickers are there to protect the manufacturer (and the salesman, and the store, and probably several other parties) from lawsuits. Now, excuse me, if I get careless and fall off a step ladder, whose fault is it? If I'm careless enough to fall off a step ladder, it seems to me it's mine. It makes no sense for me to be careless, negligent, or just plain stupid and expect someone else to pay for the damages. Yet, lawsuits have become standard procedure in this country.

My brother-in-law tells of a suit in which someone used his lawn mower for a hedge clipper and injured himself doing it. He sued and collected because the lawn mower did not have a warning that it should not be used as a hedge clipper. Was this person bright enough to draw breath? Using that line of reasoning, it would seem that lawn mowers might need warnings about not being used as toothbrushes!

I read in the local paper a story by one of the high school journalists about students not being able to use the bathrooms because the cigarette smoke is so dense—in a non-smoking high school. Why are such undisciplined individuals allowed to intrude on the rights of others in such a blatant, boorish way?

Sometimes I think that the national anthem is going to be changed into a song entitled "Oh, God, Ain't it Awful." One of the reasons people feel it's awful is that they lack the self-discipline to create the life they want for themselves. We seem to feel that we should be able to get everything we want without working for it. We want it to be easy and give up when what we need to do is redouble our efforts. We are very results conscious; we want the achievement, the success now. We usually aren't as interested in the process of how to achieve the success. The success that lotteries and gambling are having in this country attests to our desire for the getting the results without doing the time in the process of success. We love the idea of an "overnight success." What we choose to ignore is that most "overnight" successes are long, self-disciplined years in the making.

The word discipline has come to have negative connotations. Try saying the word to co-workers or friends and see what their reaction is. Most of us think of discipline as having the same appeal as scrubbing toilets—something that has to be done, but we avoid it as long as possible and hate it while we are doing it.

When we speak of disciplining children we are not usually trying to foster learning but more often trying to get them to conform. The socialization process of children also snuffs out the driving curiosity, the excitement of learning, and the pleasure of the process. Real learning requires discipline. It is the essential basis of being able to make free choices. Without self-discipline, we really don't have free choice. Without self-discipline, we are doomed to living life as children or perpetual adolescents.

The origin of the word "discipline" comes from the Latin, *discipulus*, meaning pupil. According to *The American Heritage Dictionary of the English Language,* the primary meaning of "discipline" is "training that is expected to produce a specified character or pattern of behavior, especially that which is expected to produce moral or mental improvement." Punishment is the fifth definition, yet it's the first one most people think about when they think about discipline.

Discipline is a friend, not an enemy. Discipline is an asset, not a liability. That's so much more positive. And since an undisciplined life is not worth living, it seems to me that it makes much more sense to focus on the positive aspect of discipline which is learning and mastery. Indeed, self-discipline is a requirement for living fully and richly.

TODAY'S WORLD DEMANDS SELF-DISCIPLINE

When my parents wanted a new phone, they contacted the phone company who responded by installing a black phone that was activated by an operator who answered it and said, "Number, please" (In Maine, it was really "Numbah, please"). The phone number in the farmhouse where I grew up was 224. There were no faxes, there were no answering machines, there was no circle dialing. Heck, there weren't even dials.

Today if I want a new phone, I could spend three weeks researching all the options and still not have a clear sense that I've gotten the best deal. Just as soon as I've made a choice, a new company will make another offer or one of the old ones will come out with a new plan. Now there's new information to add to an already complex set of choices. Our phone system will do much more for us today. All those options make the decision much more complex—and that's just a decision about which phone to use! The range of options and services that phone companies will offer will grow markedly in the future. This myriad of choices requires much more knowledge, thought, and decision-making. It forces me to be more self-directed and responsible.

The complexity of the world we live in is very challenging. Virtually all of the equipment in our daily lives is so much more complex than that of 50 years ago. We know so much more about everything than we did a few years ago. The pace is only going to accelerate, and the more it accelerates, the more self-responsible and self-disciplined we are going to need to be. We can't do it all, have it all, see it all, experience it all, understand it all. We are going to have to make choices. In order for the choices to be the right choices for our lives, we are going to have to be self-disciplined about acquiring the knowledge we need. We are also going to need to be self-disciplined about the choices we make with that knowledge.

For generations it has been possible to live more or less following in the footsteps of previous generations. The young boy growing up on the farm learned how to raise crops and animals from his father. Today's aspiring farmer can't get by on what his Dad knows. It's simply inadequate. The aspiring farmer better have some knowledge about genetics if he's growing tomatoes and cloning if he's raising sheep. His father may have been able to live adequately on the knowledge he inherited from his father, but the son will be required to have the self-discipline to keep up with burgeoning knowledge for the rest of his life. And so will we. We live in an exciting age of knowledge explosion All of us will need to make self-disciplined learning a focus for the rest of our lives.

That's not a problem. That's an opportunity to get back to being the learning machines we were when we were two. The best way to meet the challenges that the knowledge explosion is bringing is with the same curiosity and excitement that you brought to the world when you were two.

CHANGE AND SELF-DISCIPLINE

Human beings do not like change. There are some of us to whom the old-fashioned concept of working for one company in one job for forty years seems like a long sentence at hard labor. There are those of us who say we like change and find it stimulating and exciting. I am one of those. But, and this is a big "but," *I want to be in charge of the change.* If someone or something outside myself is directing or demanding the change, I suddenly find the change less appealing.

A few years ago I received some first-hand instruction in how change resistant I was. I had lived in one town for 15 years, but because the highway bisected the town, my mail had been delivered by the neighboring town. I returned home from work one day and opened a letter from the postmaster saying that at the end of the month, my mailing address was going to be changed. What did I, the one who thinks that change is exciting and fun, do? I went nuts! I ranted, I raved, I hooted and snorted. I made plans to write to the postmaster and call my senator. And then I realized, as I paced up and down the house that I was acting just like my Dad. I stopped mid-step and asked, "What's going on here? What is the problem?"

What was going on was "they" were changing something personal to me—my address. I wasn't concerned about the work of notifying everyone in the Universe about the change of address. I wasn't concerned about what time the mail went into the box. I didn't get home until 5 or 6 P.M., so what difference did it make? I was just howling because "they" changed something.

What I came to understand from that experience is that it is hard for us to change. It requires work. It requires a realignment of our thinking. And realigning our thinking is something that most of us are reluctant to do. The human response when confronted with new evidence about an old "truth" is to cling to the old truth—"I know what I know; don't confuse me with the facts." History is replete with examples of how most people react when confronted with new evidence. Galileo, Copernicus, and Pasteur all advanced human knowledge, brought new truth to light. Their knowledge was greeted with skepticism, derision, even outright hostility.

We now live in an era of unprecedented change, change which will continue to explode. We all need self-discipline to react and respond from the perspective of rationality and thoughtfulness. Those who get stuck in "I don't want it to be this way. Nobody told me when I was growing up I would have to prepare for five different careers over my lifetime. When can we get back to the good old days?," are as stuck as saber-toothed tigers in the La Brea tar pits. And they will meet the same fate—extinction.

William Bridges' work on the change process, as explained in *Transitions: Making Sense of Life's Changes*, is well worth studying. He suggests that every change starts with an ending. Our emotional reactions to endings are the familiar ones of denial, anger, depression, bargaining, and acceptance. During the ending stage, people are caught in and often act out of their emotions. As the change process advances, it gets more difficult to manage. The old rules no longer apply, and the new ones haven't yet been completely formulated or implemented. The hiatus causes great tension and anxiety. *What's the right thing to do? How am I supposed to act? Am I going to be able to meet the new standards? Will I like the change or hate it?* I may not have really liked the old rules, but I could take comfort in the fact that I knew them. I knew what to expect and felt comfortable in that knowledge.

Living comfortably in the turbulence of the transition requires that we detach ourselves from our emotion while at the same time being fully cognizant of what we are feeling. People who adapt successfully to change are "in touch" with their emotions but make decisions based on a rational assessment of relevant factors. They allow themselves to be conscious of their emotions but are not driven by them.

One defense against the emotion that the change arouses is to stay in denial and not let ourselves feel the impact. The more quickly one can pass through the denial stage, the more quickly one can deal with the realities of the change. I once worked in a hospital that was being sold and downsized. The staff was going to be losing jobs. Two weeks before the closing of the hospital, there were staff people who had done *nothing* about getting new employment. There were some who were simply going to collect unemployment for a period of time. That was a plan. However, there were others who simply were not dealing with the reality of their job loss. The months they had spent in denial were months in which they could have been developing strategies for developing and/or creating their next work situation. As they let time go by, they let options disappear. As options disappeared, stress and anxiety levels escalated once again, making rational decision-making less likely. In the process they became more and more overwhelmed and paralyzed by their fear. They would have been better served if they had developed the self-discipline to manage their fear and anxiety and take constructive action.

The rapidity of change no longer permits the luxury of taking time to process the feelings and move through the change stages slowly. If we spend too much time coping with one change, three more will have happened in the meantime. Persons who are so overwhelmed by one change that they can't cope are certainly going to be totally paralyzed by multiple changes. That's when people are likely going to start lamenting for the lost "good old days" when things were simpler. That, in itself, is a form of denial. Things are never going to get simpler. They are only going to become increasingly complex.

Facing fear, anxiety, anger, and distress requires self-discipline. Our natural response is to run away from those feelings. They are unpleasant and disturbing. It is so natural to pull a Scarlet O'Hara (I'll deal with it tomorrow) and today allow myself to pretend that the status is quo. The danger of this coping mechanism is that the situation usually gets worse while I stay in denial—and the situation is even harder to face and the feelings more intense. Sometimes the belief is that if I allow myself to access the feelings, they will overwhelm me. I will simply be so depressed I can't do anything. Or perhaps I'll become suicidal or murderous. The natural thing to do is to run away from the feelings, to escape.

Dealing with the situation and the feelings head on is the courageous action to take, and that requires self discipline. It is useful to ask, "What are my feelings? How am I reacting to this? Does this remind me of other situations that I've been involved in?" It is hard to do this type of work. It means we risk having to make changes within ourselves or within our relationships. If we are honest about what we think and feel, we may have to make some very hard, fundamental changes in the way we are living. The more we understand about our feelings and emotional reactions, the more ability we have to make rational decisions about how to conduct ourselves. Instead of being reactive and trying to protect ourselves from awareness of our emotions, we can be free to be proactive in making the plans and taking the steps that create the conditions in our lives that we really want.

Holding down the feelings, staying in denial, requires a lot of energy. I think that the frantic, time-driven culture we have created is partially an outgrowth of denial. We are running around madly, frantically filling up every hour of the day as a means of coping with basic, underlying unhappiness. If I let myself be still for a time, if I wasn't doing, I might be feeling.... Once the denial is exposed and we know ourselves, we are then free to utilize the energy for more productive ends.

A week before I left my marriage, I went out for a run on Thanksgiving morning. As I ran I realized that I felt wonderfully free. On asking myself what the trigger for feeling so free was, I realized that I had been expending a lot of energy trying to be happy in an unhappy situation. That had been a heavy burden I had been carrying without even noticing that I had been carrying it. The freedom was the realization that I didn't have to do that anymore. I could just be happy. The freedom was a springboard to a higher level of self-discipline. Interestingly, in the first ten months as a single woman, I finished writing a book that I had been working on for years.

I am not saying that there aren't times when it is useful to give ourselves time to absorb the impact of a change. In the face of trauma, denial can be protective in the short-term. Carried on too long, however, it becomes toxic and debilitating.

WILLINGNESS

The American Heritage Dictionary of the English Language definition of "willing" is "of or resulting from the process of choosing, volitional." When we are driven by our emotions, we cannot be volitional in our actions. We simply have less choice in our decisions. The actions that we take when driven by emotions have less potential for creating a happy ending. An unhappy husband who fears the loss of his marriage may have difficulty acknowledging his fear, sadness, and pain (after all, it's not "manly" to admit to such "weakness"). The denial of his feelings gets distorted and expressed as anger. When he acts out of the anger, he is likely acting in a way that will cause the demise of his marriage. Even if his wife doesn't divorce him, the chances of a happy marriage are destroyed. Husbands given to angry outbursts will repent afterwards and frequently say, "I don't intend to lose my temper that way. I don't know why it happens." Being driven by emotion paralyzes their ability to be volitional.

Another definition of "willing" is to be "disposed to accept." None of us can (or should) set standards for anyone else and demand compliance. Two-year olds resent demands made upon them. So do adults. As creatures of volition, each person has to be free to choose his or her own standards. You can choose to accept others for who they are and allow them the freedom to express their own unique individuality. That is not to say that you need to approve of what they are thinking, doing, or saying, just that you accept their right to be who they are. That is also not to say that you have to tolerate or condone behavior that is unacceptable to you. You can accept their behavior and your right to be absent from their behavior if that is your choice.

A third level of willingness is that of "acting or ready to act gladly." Would your life improve if you were always ready to "act gladly?" The delight of this willingness is that it automatically increases the level of joy in your life. Think about what the next twenty-four hours will be like in your life. Now, specifically think about your acting gladly throughout the next twenty-four hours. Doesn't that put a more positive spin on the coming day?

You also can choose to live out of "willingness"—to be volitional, not driven by emotion, to be more accepting of yourself and the people and situations that surround you. You will be happier and freer.

What does it take to create this type of willingness? It takes self-discipline. Does that mean I have to be perfect? Of course not. No one is—

people who seek perfectionism are invariably emotion driven. Inside them resides the belief that they have to be perfect in order to be accepted or valued. That is slavery, not freedom.

We need to re-frame the concept of self-discipline. Instead of looking at it as drudgery and punishment, we need to see it as learning. If we are **willing** to be self-disciplined, we will be **able**, able to cope effectively with the sea-change of turmoil around us, able to be self-directing in our own lives, and able to increase the enjoyment and pleasure of our lives. Self-discipline is the key to being free. The unself-disciplined live in conditions of slavery, bondage of their own creation.

Action Steps

1. Number a sheet of paper from 1 - 10. Without stopping to think, quickly write ten times, "If I were more self-disciplined, I..."
2. Pick one aspect of your life that you would like to improve, for example, fitness or financial well-being. Visualize what your results would be if you were self-disciplined in that area.
3. Choose an area you wish to improve and ask yourself how your thoughts or behavior would change if you were more self-disciplined. Write a list of actions or thoughts that would meet that goal. Do them!
4. Assess your level of pride in yourself on a 1 - 10 scale. Do a global pride scale—an overall rating of yourself. Then rate yourself on specific areas—career, fitness, appearance, energy level, financial fitness etc. Select as many areas as you wish. Ask yourself how ratings would change if you were more self-disciplined.
5. Flex your change muscles often. Try on clothes that are totally different from the styles you normally buy. Eat different foods. Try a new hobby. Learn a new skill or craft.

Points to Ponder

- How you view the future determines how you live today. How you live today determines your future.
- Responsibility is freedom.
- An effort a day keeps the failure away.
- Unexpressed, undealt with "negative" emotions like fear, anger, and pain grow larger and create boils of the spirit. Faced and dealt with, they diminish. Unexpressed "positive" emotions—love, compassion, and joy—

grow smaller. Expressed, they expand.
- Don't spend your time, invest it.
- If you cannot control yourself, your actions and emotions, you will be victimized—by yourself.
- If you can control your mind, you can control your world.
- Think joyfully—Act gladly.

Chapter 4

TAKING STOCK, THE FIRST STEP IN TAKING CHARGE OF YOUR LIFE

FOR MORE YEARS than I care to remember, I lived in a marriage that was not happy. We didn't fight. We got along reasonably well. Other people looked at us and thought that we had a great relationship. But we didn't. We were living in well-orchestrated roles of the happily married couple, but we weren't happy. The life and vitality of our relationship had slowly diminished over the years while we were engrossed in working and raising children. The anger built up—in both of us. The issues that divided us and separated us were never talked about. Although married, we were alone. If you had asked me if I was angry I'd have said, "No." Disappointed, hurt, sad, yes. But, angry, not me.

When I was forty, I looked at my marriage and said to myself, "There's no intimacy in my marriage." Then I looked around and said, "There's no intimacy in anybody else's marriage either. I guess I'll just make do with creating intimacy with my women friends and not worry about what's missing in my marriage." And then, I promptly went back into denial. A few years later, suffering from trigeminal neuralgia, an excruciatingly painful facial syndrome, I asked myself, "What is the metaphor that my body is expressing? What is painful for me to face?" My answer was, it was painful for me to face the fact that I was not happy in my marriage. And then I went promptly back into denial. Where did I learn to go unconscious with my anger? Where did I learn to put myself in denial? Right at my mother's knee. My maternal grandmother died long before I was born, but I have no doubts that my mother learned it from her mother. Interestingly enough, I do not remember ever being told not to be angry and that I shouldn't be angry. In fact, I remember my mother telling me when I was angry to "go out and run around the house until you feel better." She didn't deny me my right to be angry or tell me I shouldn't feel angry because it wasn't nice. She even gave me sound physiological advice about what to do with the energy of my anger.

She also gave me very powerful role modeling about how a woman was supposed to act—and it never included speaking up for herself. It never included expressing anger. I remember how my father used to come into the kitchen, expecting to have dinner on the table (a common experience for children growing up in the fifties) and expressing impatience when it wasn't ready. I remember how angry I felt toward his boorish insensitivity. After all, my mother was mothering a brood of nine children in very pressured economic circumstances and working forty hours a week in a local restaurant as a cook. Why couldn't he lift a hand and do something to get his own dinner?

In addition to the direct example laid down by my mother and the mothers of my friends, the culture was at work, subtly teaching me that it wasn't nice to be angry. My church taught me that it was a sin and that I could go to hell for being angry. My older brother who resented me intensely and teased and taunted me throughout my childhood taught me that it was dangerous to express my anger or retaliate. Whenever I did, I ended up getting pounded.

When I was in eighth grade, Sam Wescott was teasing me one afternoon on the bus trip home from school. His target? My weight. Bullies always know where the vulnerabilities are. I told him several times to stop. When the teasing continued, I told him that I was going to beat him up if he didn't stop. He persisted so I carried through with my threat and beat him up. Instead of feeling good that justice had been served and that the bully had been stopped, I was humiliated and embarrassed. I was particularly embarrassed because of my empathy for Sam's feelings. I felt really bad about his humiliation. How awful to be beaten up by a girl.

It wasn't until I was an adult that I realized that my anger was justified and that Sam's humiliation was a direct result of his behavior, not mine. If he was humiliated, he deserved it. As an adult I recognized that it would have been just for me to walk away from that fight saying, "He got what he deserved and maybe next time he'll think twice about being a bully."

My socialization in going underground with my anger was complete. I had learned to punish myself for righteous expression of my anger. It is not surprising that one of the most difficult things for me was directly expressing my anger at a male. It wasn't nice, and it was too dangerous. Until I was willing to consciously own my anger and express it as an adult, I was limited *by my efforts to be in an authentic relationship with another. I wasn't in an authentic relationship with myself.*

Recovering the connection to our authentic selves requires a brutal honesty with ourselves about who we are, who we've been, and who we want to be. As nations are doomed to repeat their history unless they study it and understand it, so are we as individuals. Until we are able and willing to face the pain, anger, injustice, and suffering that all of us have experienced in one form or another, we will keep blundering into the same scenarios again and again. Only by breaking through the denial do we stand a chance of getting free to really experience ourselves.

The decision to change and express ourselves more directly, honestly, and openly does not get taken lightly by the people around us. People close to us can become very unnerved when we change. When I was a clinician working with overweight women, I observed how powerful this dynamic can be. My clients were usually women who had been obese for a number of years. Most of them had tried every diet known to woman without success. While they were on Optifast and losing regularly, many of them began to appear to be making a permanent change in their body weight.

When that happened, the people around them began to come out of the woodwork and start to lobby for regaining the weight. Husbands, perhaps threatened that their wives were going to become thinner and more sexually attractive, would suddenly start bringing home Godiva chocolates. Co-workers, who had enjoyed the obese woman's lack of assertiveness and willingness to do the tasks in the office that no one else wanted to do, began issuing lunch invitations and being seductive and manipulative with comments like, "You never go out to lunch with us anymore. This one time won't hurt." Friends who were struggling with their own weight problems became jealous.

One woman reported that her grandson said to her, "I liked you better when you were fat. Grandmothers are supposed to be soft." Another told the story of picking her preschool child up after class and having the child say to her,"You don't look like my mother anymore." How totally disconcerting to have your mother change so much that you hardly recognize her! Still another who had a very supportive husband and child and who has sustained a 160 pound weight loss for many years now cut her hair several months after she finished losing weight. Her ten year old son confided in her, "I want you to grow your hair back. It's the only thing that was the same."

Do you remember when you were a child and Great Aunt Tillie who hadn't seen you for a year came to visit? Do you remember standing there while she gushed, "Oh! My! How you've grown!"? I remember standing in the front yard of my house while my grandparents and aunts did that routine. I loved it when they came to visit, but I *hated* the "My how you've changed" routine. I can remember saying to myself, "Well, of course, I've grown. I'm a kid and that's what kids do—grow!" I vowed to myself that when I grew up I would never say that to a kid. And then I grew up and had nieces and nephews visit that I hadn't seen for a long time. Before I could snap my lips shut the words whistled out of my mouth, "My! How you've grown!"

When I asked myself why I had broken my vow, the only reasonable explanation was that the miracle of the growth of a child is so remarkable, so astonishing—even though we've seen it and experienced it all of our lives—that we spontaneously express our wonder at the process. It is unbelievable that children change so much. We just can't incorporate so much change all at once. When the children live with us and we see the change unfold, it seems normal. When we are presented with such profound changes all at once, we can't incorporate the reality—and the words declare, "How you've changed."

The changes in our children also bluntly remind us of the passage of time. I look at my adult children and I can't believe that I'm old enough to have kids that old. I still feel like a twenty-year old in my mind. The fact that my older son is in his late twenties presents the reality of time gone by. On one hand, I like the adult man he has become. On the other, I miss the days when both of us were younger and shared more of each other's daily lives. Change always causes ambivalence.

When anyone changes, it causes dis-ease and anxiety in the people around them. We delude ourselves in thinking that there is safety in stability. There is not. The safety is only an illusion, a Linus blanket that we use to allow ourselves to feel more comfortable. When we start changing, we are in effect taking someone else's blanket away from them.

There are unwritten, often unspoken, rules that govern the behavior of people in a group. Almost every household occupied by more than one person has a morning shower schedule. Everyone knows what time each person is going to be in the shower. Mom is expected to be in the shower at "her" time, Dad his, and the children theirs. This schedule was probably not negotiated or overtly decided upon. It evolved and everyone understands it and usually abides by it. Great consternation arises when someone moves into someone else's place. Then the steam in the bathroom really rises!

Work groups also have their unwritten rules. They aren't part of the orientation to the job, and they don't exist in the policy and procedure manuals, but they are a real and vital part of the way the groups work—or don't work—together. They are powerful. The company manual (and the unwritten family manual) may, for example say that we believe in honesty. Too often, the real rule is that we are honest, but.... There are some things that we don't say, even though in their hearts everyone recognizes the truth.

It is more difficult to change the unwritten, unspoken rules than it is the conscious ones. The woman who begins to say, in word or deed, "I'm not longer willing to tolerate your excessive drinking," or the man who says, "I'm not happy in my job, I need to make a change," is changing the unwritten rules. The woman is challenging the loving, supportive female image, and the man is challenging the male as breadwinner rule. As a society, it has become easier over the past several decades to challenge the underlying rules. On an individual level, it causes turmoil within ourselves and within those around us while the change is happening.

If you want to test this theory, try the following experiment. Sit at someone else's place at the table at dinner some night and watch the dynamics in action. We simply do not like it when people we are close to change. It threatens our sense of safety, security, and comfort. It takes courage to come out of denial and start openly expressing yourself—even to yourself. We fear that all hell will break loose if we let ourselves become conscious. For that reason all too many people decide, consciously or unconsciously, that they are not going to rock the boat. The dreadful result of that decision is that we are then greasing the skids of our relationships with our self-esteem and our integrity. We are making a decision to live inauthentically—a decision that cannot help but reduce the quality of our lives.

When I was first married, my mother-in-law did not like me. I was not the woman that she wanted her first-born to marry. She was rude and obnoxious to me on many occasions. I, for reasons that are very clear to you, did not defend myself or tell her off. I told myself that it was not all that important, that I did not see her all that often, and I could handle it. Needless to say, her visits were not a lot of fun.

When my first son was three months old, we took him to visit his Grandmother for the first time. As we sat at the picnic table on a glorious summer afternoon eating lunch just prior to our departure, my husband reached for the potato salad. His mother reprimanded him for not asking for it to be passed, then made a snide comment about how good his manners had been prior to his marriage. For some reason that comment took me over the edge. Without losing control, I picked up my baby and told my husband that I would be waiting in the car whenever he was ready. And I told my mother-in-law that I was not going to tolerate her obnoxious behavior ever again. I announced emphatically but politely, that when Adam was old enough to travel with his father, I would not stop him from visiting, but I personally did not intend to return.

What a gloriously freeing declaration of independence! What a profound statement of my demand to be treated with respect. What wonderful SELF assertion! I couldn't believe how good it felt to state my position after several years of taking her subtle—and not so subtle—abuse. I wish I could say that as a result of that episode our relationship became close and supportive. It never did, but at least I was never treated as badly again.

What I learned from the experience was that it was not good for either of us for me to remain silent while she verbally insulted me. I had been sacrificing my self-esteem in the hopes that if I was "good enough" she would come to see what a valuable person I was. I had been letting this unhappy woman suck the blood out of my self-esteem. Not only did I need to get out of my denial about how badly I was being treated, I needed to act in my own behalf. And I never again let her anger, hostility, and pain take big bites out of my self-esteem.

The intense anger that I felt that day was a gift. It took me beyond the reach of all my socialization about being "nice." It took me beyond my fears of, and distaste for, upsetting other people. It took me out of my pathological denial into a place where I could act with integrity and demand justice.

None of us escapes childhood without having shut down and chopped off pieces of ourselves in an effort to please and comply. We go along to get along. As children we are completely dependent on the adults around us. In addition, adult approval feels really good. We learn to hide the pieces of ourselves that won't be approved. We learn to hide from others, and we learn to hide from ourselves. Until we are willing to go back and re-examine those pieces of ourselves, we are caught in their clutches, doomed to endlessly repeat the pattern. When life brings us to a point of touching upon those issues, we tend to react with anxiety and fear. I'd rather see myself as a calm, gentle, peaceful, and loving person than an angry bitch. The trouble is the angry bitch is just as much a part of me as my toes. And until I own her and embrace her and accept that she is me, I will inevitably contaminate my relationships with the anger.

My anger is just as legitimate and real as my love. Until I'm willing to accept that, I am doomed to living as fragmented and broken. Only through breaking out of my denial can I re-establish the integrity of my self. Only when I am truly integrated as a whole person am I truly capable of loving anyone else. Breaking out of denial is the most loving thing that you can do, either for yourself or for another.

One of the fears we have about coming out is that the negative parts of ourselves, those disowned pieces of ourselves will take over and run amok. We fear that we will lose control and destroy everything in sight. The truth is, people who recognize and own the "less than savory" parts of themselves are not the ones who go up in the tower and lay waste with machine guns. Going "postal" is the outgrowth of denial. Healthy expression of anger prevents out-of-control eruptions of violence.

Sexuality is another issue that it is still hard for us to come clean on. Although we are more open about sexuality now than in the fifties when I was a teenager, we still are in denial about how totally sexual we are. When we acknowledge, usually secretly, that we think our best friend's husband has a wonderful butt and start to think about what it looks like or feels like and start to get aroused by the thoughts, we shut down telling ourselves that we don't feel it. We are lying. And in the lie, we cut ourselves off from parts of ourselves.

One of the most outrageous, totally messed up things that the

Catholic church of my youth taught me was that it "was as bad to think it as to do it." I can remember feeling so debased and humiliated in the confessionals of Saturday afternoon, confessing to "impure thoughts." Masturbation was euphemized to "impure actions with myself." They messed with me so badly that I couldn't even say that I was thinking about sex and enjoying it and getting aroused! They messed with me so badly I couldn't enjoy my body without feeling debased and guilty. Impure thoughts! Impure actions! What rubbish!

What I was experiencing was a healthy, wonderful aspect of my humanity. They kept me from knowing that my sexual thoughts, feelings, and desires were normal and healthy, that thoughts about sex and the pleasure it brings are a part of my birthright as a human being. They didn't keep me from knowing the pleasure that self-stimulation brings, but they sure did make me feel guilty about it. What I now know is that if God had intended for humans not to masturbate, human genitals would be located in the middle of our backs and our arms would be short!

Men still hide their Playboys—maybe not from their wives and friends, but from their children. Or they keep their porno videos locked up. In the meantime the average child is free to view all sorts of murder and mayhem on television. The underlying message is: Violence is socially acceptable. Sexual feelings and curiosity should be hidden and denied.

The truth is, we are still in denial about how central sexuality is to our thoughts. We're still stuck in the "it's as bad to think it as it is to do it" mentality. We fear that if we really acknowledged and owned all of our sexuality we'd become out-of-control sex-crazed monsters. The truth is that the people who are in denial of their sexuality are the ones who break out and transgress against others. Catholic priests who seem to have a predilection for young boys are a prime example here. Their code is institutionalized denial of sexuality. They vow to be non-sexual. That makes as much sense as taking a vow to be non-breathing. I'm not saying we don't have a right to express our sexuality or not express it if that is our choice, but to be in denial about it is not only a diminution of the totality of our person, it is too often downright dangerous for others.

CHARLIE'S DILEMMA

Charlie is in his late forties, a very successful businessman who enjoys all the toys that nearly unlimited wealth can buy. He has both southern and northern beach homes, art work, collections, and the opportunity to attend the high profile sporting events that he loves. He is busy constantly, moving frenetically from activity to activity. Underneath this activity and accomplishment is a deep and searing pain.

He has had a string of marital infidelities. He is dissatisfied with his sex life but maintains that he loves his wife and will never divorce her. He is overweight. He drinks too much. His children are talented and handsome. One of them is an accomplished athlete. The other excels at music. Both attend prestigious private schools. One of them has a problem with alcohol and has been picked up for driving under the influence.

Charlie is very thoughtful and perceptive. He is an affectionate, loving man who yearns for deep and profound connection to those he loves. He is, however, "looking for love in all the wrong places." He is looking outward. Where he needs to look is inward. He needs to know about the pain from which he is fleeing with so much energy and determination. He needs to know what he is denying. Until he does, he will remain spinning in his cycle of misery, whirling about his life trying to keep the awareness from surfacing.

The lifestyle that he has chosen will shorten his life. The life he is living is hollow and deep down he knows it. Nothing will improve—indeed it will further deteriorate—until he is able to stop doing what he is doing, and take a good, long, hard, introspective look at the totality of who he is, the choices he has made, and the totality of the life he lives. Only when, and if, he makes that hard, courageous choice does he stand a chance of breaking free of the trap he is in. Only the light of truth slowly and thoroughly illuminating the entire landscape of his life can bring him out of his own darkness and into the peace and calm he needs.

TAKING CHARGE

When we take charge of the parts of us that we are in denial about, when we allow ourselves to become conscious about the denied "self," then we are in a position to be thoughtful and rational about how, or if, we take action on our insights. Until we are conscious, we are in danger of being driven and controlled by the denied experiences and feelings. Until we are conscious, we don't control our experiences. They control us.

Another area that tends to be clouded with denial is that of our specialness, our uniqueness. If we are lucky, we are born to a mother (and even better, a father, too) who from the earliest days of our lives talks to us and demonstrates to us that we are important. The parents saying in word and deed, "We adore you, you are wonderful, you are special, never has there been anyone as wonderful as you" is the lullaby on which strong, healthy self-esteem is built.

Even for those of us who got that foundation laid, the encounters with the world soon separate us from the recognition of our uniqueness. We are urged, encouraged, pushed, and directed to conform by the larger world. And parents, as we discussed in an earlier chapter, become a powerful pressure source for us to conform.

Last summer a speaker colleague approached me and asked if he could give me some feedback. It was obvious from his manner that he felt like he was taking a risk. I said, "Yes, of course." The feedback he gave me was, "Rita, I think you should own your own greatness more than you do." That was a most wonderful gift. I've given a great deal of thought about that comment in the months since. He was right. I was denying just how creative, insightful, beautiful, capable, and strong I really am.

What I learned through his comment was that it is just as debilitating and dangerous to deny the "wonderful" parts of ourselves as it is to disown the "bad" parts of ourselves. In either case what I am doing is denying myself the ability to be integrated, conscious, and whole.

As I thought about why I disowned my greatness, several insights arose. First of all, powerful women can be source of fear. People tend to dislike them and label them less than flattering terms like "aggressive" or "bitch." Men are intimidated by them and other women resent them. So, how would you like to be alone and not understood? The fear I found at the bottom is that of being alone. However, denying who I am to myself, and consequently to others, leaves me alone anyhow. In order to be truly connected, I must be acting out of integrity. Genuine connection with others can only occur when I am perceived accurately for who I am. When my connection to others is based on a facade, the relationship is a facade. In the final analysis for me, being alone as an integrated, healthy human being is preferable to being separated from my self, or living life as a facade.

I thought about where I had learned to disown my greatness and remembered childhood friends cautioning me about letting others know how many A's I got on my report card. It would make them feel bad. The flaw in this reasoning was that my grades had any connection to the others. I remembered hearing that "nobody likes a braggart." Other comments like "don't toot your own horn" and "Who do you think you are, smarty pants?" were enough to tell me that the reason I didn't own my greatness was that I had been taught not to. And I decided that I could unlearn it just as well. Now I sit here at the computer with visions of my book on *The New York Times* bestseller list, and I love the idea!

You, too, have a capacity for greatness. You, too, have a song to sing. Right now, your vocal cords may be weak, and you may need voice lessons but the capacity is there for you to release. If you don't bring it to light, the light will never shine. No one else can do it for you. It is your task, your challenge, your delight.

The reality is that there has never been a person just like you, ever, in the history of the world. There never will be again. When seen from that perspective, you are indeed special. And the vast majority of us live our entire lives never acknowledging or knowing this. And when we stay in denial of our uniqueness, we deny ourselves and the world the unique gifts that we might bring. How many brilliant scientists have died without ever setting foot inside a lab because they got scripted to become postmen? How many poems have gone unwritten because the poet was told that she needed to make sure she had a secure job? How many songs have gone unsung because the songwriter was told that it was too difficult to get published? Are you willing to let the same tragic fate befall you? I hope not! If you've read this far, there is a voice within you, a faint one perhaps, but a voice within you that is longing to speak. There is joy, and laughter, beauty, and freedom that the world needs to hear. And there is joy, laughter, beauty, and freedom that is yours, and yours, alone to express.

Action Steps

1. Brian Tracy poses a wonderful, terrifying question in one of his *Insight Series* audiotapes: "What is now present in your life that you wouldn't choose today?" If there are obligations or commitments that you would not agree to today, what are they? Spend as much time as you need exploring these issues on paper. Just writing them

Unlock Your Possibilities

down does not mean that you are going to blow up your landscape and destroy everyone and everything in sight. Getting the goblins out into the light of consciousness means that you are then in a position to rationally and thoughtfully make decisions about what is the best course of action for you.

You may not have a perfect course of action open to you. No one ever does. The decisions that you make may cause pain to others. It is highly likely that your denial is already causing pain so pain avoidance is no reason to skip this exercise. Overcoming denial is essential to your health. Only when you are healthy can you bring health to others.

2. In order for your life to be different in the future, you must change things in your life today. It is usually fear that keeps us from moving, growing, or changing. List as many fears as you can about what would happen if you changed. As you do this exercise, write quickly, don't censor or edit as you write. Let the thoughts flow.

3. In order to keep things in perspective, write out your fears about the future you will have if you don't change.

4. Please fill out the following checklist.

FEELING GOOD CHECKLIST

In the space provided, list the activities that make you feel good or not good about yourself. It doesn't matter if you have more or fewer items than ten.

I FEEL GOOD ABOUT MYSELF WHEN

1. _____
_____
2. _____
_____
3. _____
_____
4. _____
_____
5. _____
_____
6. _____
_____

7. _____
8. _____
9. _____
10. _____

I FEEL NOT GOOD ABOUT MYSELF WHEN

1. _____
2. _____
3. _____
4. _____
5. _____
6. _____
7. _____
8. _____
9. _____
10. _____

Look at the lists and place a check beside those items that have happened in the last two weeks, then indicate the number of times the event has occurred during that time frame. Analyze the list to determine whether you control each event or someone else does. For example, if you wrote "spouse complimented me," that is an other-controlled event.

| UNLOCK YOUR POSSIBILITIES |

For each other-controlled event, place an "O" beside the item. for each self-controlled event, place an "S" beside the item.

NEXT, COMPARE THE TWO LISTS. CONSIDER THE FOLLOWING QUESTIONS:

Do you see patterns?
Have you deprived yourself of activities that make you feel good?
Can you increase the frequency of "feel good" events?
Can you decrease the frequency of "not good" events?
Are you feeling bad about yourself as a result of the actions of others?
If so, does it make sense to allow that to continue to happen?

5. Sentence completions are an excellent tool for isolating the denial spots in our lives. Thinking of this journey into and through your denial as a detective story is an excellent idea. This is an Agatha Christie mystery—who/what killed that beautiful, unique self that you are? When you know who/what perpetrated the crime you get to change the script into a love story—for yourself!

FREE-ASSOCIATE, PREFERABLY IN WRITING, TO THE FOLLOWING STIMULUS PHRASES:

1. I wish I...
2. The hardest thing for me is...
3. Heaven, for me, would be...
4. My mother hated (hates)...
5. If I could be an animal, I'd like to be...
6. A secret I'd hesitate to tell anyone is...
7. One of the most exciting experiences of my childhood was...
8. If I could be a kid again, I'd...
9. One of the biggest regrets I have is...
10. My favorite comfort food is...
11. I'm ashamed of...
12. If I'd had a perfect childhood I...
13. Something I like about the holidays is...
14. Something I dislike about the holidays is...
15. My life is...

16. My life will be...

6. One of my favorite *Artist's Way* (by Julia Cameron) exercises is to write down five of your secret selves. If you could live five secret lives, who would you be? Write them down and then describe what each of them would have in their closets. My own secret selves include Regina, the queen, Thea, the Greek Goddess, Snarly, the witch, and Trudy, the Tramp.

Points to Ponder

- The ultimate lesson that all of us have to learn is unconditional love, which includes not only others but ourselves as well.
  — Elisabeth Kübler-Ross
- Honest arrogance is better than hypocritical humility. — Alan Weiss
- When you are angry at the world—or yourself—don't turn on those who love you, turn to them.
- To live, not just exist, we need to constantly reinvent ourselves.
- You cannot get to where you are going if you refuse to leave where you are.
- Once severed from the future, the past becomes an insignificant parade of trivial events, no longer organic, no longer potent or painful.
  — Trevanian

Chapter 5

COMING TO YOUR SENSES: STAYING IN YOUR RIGHT MIND

THE CHILL LEFT by the night raised tiny tendrils of fog from the surface of the Vermont lake. I stood on the shore shivering in the cool morning air. I was ready for this race and enjoying the sights and sounds of the pre-race activities—friends greeting each other, the splash of swimmers in the water as they warmed up, the golden-orange color of the early sun hitting the trees on the opposite shore. The lake surface was calm, disturbed only by the strokes of the swimmers and an occasional bird settling into the water. I felt vibrantly alive and eager for the fun of the race to begin. I was anticipating the pleasures of tapping into my physical strength, my technical mastery of the swimming, biking, and running skills, and the joy of the flow state created by racing.

The first waves of racers were summoned to the starting line, and I watched as they ran into the water, whooping with enthusiasm, splashing a wake pattern into the surface of the lake. Soon each pack looked like a bizarre school of fish, flailing across the water. I moved into place, feeling the cool wet sand beneath my feet. I pulled my goggles into place, making sure they were snug and water-tight. As the starter called out, "On your mark," I tensed my body and couched slightly, preparing to sprint for the water. "Get set." I set my mind and focused on getting off smoothly and easily. "Go." I burst into motion running easily at first, then slowing as I encountered the resistance of the deepening water. Cool water seeped into my wetsuit. The efficiency of running diminished. I raised my feet and began to swim.

The first few yards of the swim were difficult as I physically and mentally geared up. In the lag between the start and achieving swimming efficiency, it was easy to start to feel apprehensive and uneasy. I wanted to stay relaxed, *knowing that apprehension was a zapper of efficiency and effectiveness. "Just stay focused on your swim stroke. Don't pay any attention to those swimming around you. Get the maximum pull from your right hand. Now, insert your left hand into the water at just the right angle, follow with a smooth, powerful stroke." I moved into overdrive, swimming smoothly and enjoying the sleek, powerful feel of my motion through the water.*

Now I could look around and see if there was a pair of feet I could hook onto—a swimmer that I could tail taking advantage of the hydrodynamic boost that tailing someone would provide. It's the same principle as the v-formation of a flock of geese. The trailing geese don't have to work as hard as the lead goose. I found my feet and enjoyed the prowess that enabled me to take advantage of drafting another swimmer.

Now I was halfway through the swim course. Suddenly I noticed that my focus had shifted, and I was thinking about the "killer" hill that I was going to have to run at mile five of the run. Wow! That hill was long and steep. By the time I got there, the day was going to be hot and humid. I found myself dreading that hill.

And then I caught myself. What was I doing, worrying about the run when I was in the water? Was it doing me any good? No! Indeed, it was harming my race effort. It was dragging me down, sapping my energy and my confidence. I told myself that I didn't need to worry about that hill. No sense worrying about it until I got there. As a matter of fact, there wasn't any sense worrying about it when I got there either. I was just going to run it as efficiently as I could. It would be easy or hard, it didn't make any difference. I was going to do it.

The next question I asked myself was "What do you need to do right now?" The answer was "Right now, I need to focus on what I am doing. I need to give my full attention, my full effort to swimming." I moved back into the moment, full awareness, once again enjoying the sleek, powerful feel of my body moving through the water.

Later, at mile five of the run, I mastered the hill, not without effort and focus, but I ran up and over it, just as I had run up and over the anxiety of worrying about it.

The headlong pace of our lives finds us racing through endless activities without really being present in any of the moments. While I am talking to a friend, it is all too easy to start thinking about the "to-do" list, or associating something she has said with another memory, or being distracted by the external noises I'm hearing outside the office. I have become partially disconnected from my friend. I'm not really there when part of me is somewhere else. Too many of us spend most of our lives "somewhere else."

The complexity of our lives makes it more difficult to be here, fully present in the now. We attempt to get twenty-six hours of activity into every twenty-four. The treadmills that most of us live on are set at a fast pace. We get up in the morning and race through the "getting-out-the-door" routine, making sure that the kids have their lunches and homework, getting ourselves ready (I have discovered that I am not the only one who has arrived at work and discovered that I was wearing one navy shoe and one black shoe), dashing madly into the traffic chaos and sitting in traffic, roaring through a frantic day at work where the pile on the desk keeps growing no matter how fast we turn it over, racing home to toss a quick dinner on the table and then dashing off to a child's soccer game or a school function. Our "leisure" time in the evening is spent making sure the homework is done and catching up on the laundry and perhaps an entertaining round of bill-paying, after which we fall into bed, hurrying to get to sleep so that we don't miss the early alarm. The next day is a Xerox copy. The days fly by. Life flies by.

It is so easy to be distracted. We move so quickly through life's moments that we have little conscious "life" in our moments. So life goes by in a blur and the landscape is not clearly visible. We lose sight of the fact that these moments *are* our lives. As Deepak Chopra has observed, we need to go from being nowhere to "now here." We need to go from being mindless to being mindful. Paying attention is a critical life skill. Spending time without paying full attention is like spending five dollars and being satisfied with two dollars worth of value.

While I was swimming and worrying about the run, I was not totally present to the activity in which I had chosen to engage. I needed to become aware that I had slipped out of the now before I could course-correct and get back into mindfulness. I needed to register what was happening to me and come to my senses.

Recently, I was out running on a beautiful spring morning. As I ran I was aware of the sound of my breathing and the sounds of my footsteps and the delicious background music of the birds busily telling the exuberant tales of spring. I was aware of the feeling of my breath as it moved in and out of my body. I was aware of the smooth powerful motion of the muscles of my legs and the sensations of easy, rhythmical flow as I moved. I was also aware of different temperatures as I moved in and out of patches of the early morning sun. How delicious the warmth of that sunshine felt! I noticed the dappling of the light patterns on the leaves and the bright, vibrant green of the fresh new leaves that decked the trees. I noticed the different shades of green, the lighter shades of the birches and the deep mature green of the pines. I noticed the light-colored tips on the evergreens, signs of new growth. I inhaled deeply the fragrances around me. The deep scent of lilacs delighted me as did the lush smell of lilies-of-the-valley. I watched birds flying near me and observed a tiny chipmunk lecturing me from his perch on the stone wall. All around me was the visual feast of spring blossoms. I was aware as I ran that I was richly connected to my senses and that I felt really alive, vibrantly, richly alive. I was connected to my self and my senses. I felt unified and whole—at one with myself and the world in which I live.

I run or walk most mornings. Many times, I am less in my senses. I let my mind drift, allowing the thoughts to come and go as they will. I don't have vivid memories of many of my runs. I don't always run as consciously as I did that day. It is interesting to observe that my pleasure in that run was intensified, both as I ran it and as I remember it. The difference between that run and many of my runs is that I was "in my senses," focused on the multiple levels of experience I was having simultaneously. I was more conscious, more alive.

During that run, I wasn't thinking about what I had to do that day. I wasn't rehashing old hurt feelings and discontents, focused on the past. I wasn't concerned about the future, worrying about how I was going to find the time to finish the book, pay the mortgage, or even wondering what I was going to eat for breakfast when I finished running. I was with myself and the experiences of that moment.

How much of your time do you spend mindlessly moving from activity to activity without giving a thought to what is happening in the moment? I think about the times that I have driven home and on arrival realized that I had no recollection of the drive home. I'd been "on automatic." Our capacity for going on automatic makes us very efficient. Because I don't have to attend fully to the routine aspects of my day it is possible to get many more things accomplished. The downside is that it makes it possible for us to live unfocused, lifeless lives.

There is an inherent tug between the efficiency of being on automatic and the enhanced vibrancy of being fully focused in our senses. In order to have the best possible life, we need to be able to shift easily back and forth, getting maximum gain from both states. Nathaniel Branden, writing in *The Art of Living Consciously* states it succinctly: "If we want to be effective, we need to learn what to pay attention to, and what to leave 'on automatic'."

Far too many of us are stuck in mindlessness. The billions of hours of television watching, going to the movies, and attending spectator sports are mostly spent mindlessly. Is it possible to be mindful while watching television or movies? Yes, of course, but it requires paying attention—deciding to be actively engaged in reacting to and thinking about the story being told. Is there benefit from the fabulous technology of our movies and entertainment opportunities? Of course, it allows us to experience things that we could never experience otherwise. The danger is that instead of using them as tools for enhancing our experience, our understanding, or growth, and our pleasure, we mindlessly use them as a sleeping pill, numbing us from the experience of our real lives.

There is value in not thinking about the separate steps involved in the actions I take while I am showering or cooking dinner. I can get real value from the random thoughts that occur in the shower. Some valuable insights and pleasurable thoughts are available to me that I couldn't access if I had to focus on whether I washed my left arm first or the right. I can enhance my enjoyment of cooking dinner while carrying on a conversation with a family member. Because I can split my focus, I can live on multiple levels simultaneously.

I also get real value from the experience of standing in the shower and being totally mindful of that experience, feeling the luscious sensations of hot water cascading over my body, smelling the scent of the shampoo, and feeling the stimulation of the loofah on my skin. I can relax into the sensations and let them totally fill the moment. I feel a sense of deep gratitude for living in a place and time where I can shower every day, even twice a day if I so choose. I recognize that I am statistically in a very rare place. The vast majority of human beings who have ever lived haven't ever had the experience, the total delight and luxury of a hot shower, not even once. And I can do it every day!

Our culture values doing much more than being. There are more direct rewards for those who are productive *doers* than there are for those who are adept at *being*. Indeed it is easy to see those who focus on being as wastrels, goof offs who don't justify their existence. We seem to have the belief that it's an either/or proposition; either I'm a doer, a productive good person who doesn't "waste" a minute or I'm an idler, a mediator who sits around contemplating my navel and wasting my life. The Western way of thought values the doing. Our incredible wealth and marvelous technology is a testimony to the value of that type of thinking. The Eastern mode of thought values the being and the peace and tranquility that can be achieved through that type of mindfulness has its own value. The delight of our times is the growing recognition that we can have both. It is not an either/or proposition. The real value lies in developing both capacities. In the integration, there is a fuller realization and development of our humanness. By the integration, we move human consciousness to a new level. We participate in the continuing evolution of the human species.

My own personal experience verifies the value of integrating both ways of being. I have moved from being totally immersed in the Western mode of thought to an understanding and valuing of Eastern ways of thought. The time and space I have given in my life to being, to practicing yoga, and meditation has not reduced my productivity. Indeed, the opposite has happened! I am more productive, more creative, and happier today than I have ever been. I feel more grounded in my being and at the same time freer than I ever have been. But don't take my word for it. Experiment yourself. Take the time and develop your "being" and see what happens in your own life.

How do we "come to our senses" and begin to live more mindfully and vibrantly? We learn. In this case it's not a matter of learning a new skill; it's a matter of reconnecting to abilities you once had. It's allowing your two-year old to come out and play more often. It's a matter of deciding to be more focused on each moment of your life, to pay more attention to the fact that life swirls in multiple levels in, through, and around you. It is noticing that you are marvelously and wonderfully connected to it all. One suggestion is to ask yourself periodically during the day to pay attention. Right now, notice how the chair or couch feels under your body, become aware of how the book feels as you hold it. What can you smell? Are there sounds in your environment? Notice your breathing. How does your breath feel as it moves in and out of your body? Are there places of tension in your body or is it really relaxed?

I was lucky with regard to being aware of my surroundings. My mother was, and is, tuned in to, aware of, and appreciative of the natural world around her. She is given to exclaiming, frequently exclaiming, "Isn't that beautiful?" as she observes the world around her. Without ever saying to me, "Rita, pay attention; notice the details of the world around you," she taught me how to do just that. It was, and is, a wonderful gift of life to my life.

STAYING IN YOUR RIGHT MIND—PHYSIOLOGICALLY

As Westerners, we have for centuries focused on, and valued rational thinking, linear thought, and logic. We've placed more value on left-brain thinking than on right-brain thinking. Our education system has been almost totally devoted to the development of our left-brains. We've been taught to revere the facts, completely denying that what we now believe are facts were once ideas that existed only in someone's imagination. When I was in high school I learned that there were nine planets, that girls didn't have the stamina to play full-court basketball, and that the Russians were my mortal enemies.

Sputnik shocked me and unnerved me (and my contemporaries). It was totally at odds with what I "knew." It was a signal that there was a different perspective. It signaled that what we "knew" was not necessarily the whole story. The expectation that had been created by my childhood was that knowledge was stable. I didn't expect, or imagine, that life would change so radically over my lifetime. As I contemplate what life will be like over the next fifty years, I get excited—and a little uneasy. I haven't yet learned how to program my VCR; will I be able to run my kitchen appliances in the year 2048? Will I even need kitchen appliances in 2048? Perhaps I'll get my food in some way that I can't even imagine at this juncture.

All the wonderful, technological marvels that we use every day are the result of someone's "playing" with ideas, of asking "what if?" Thinking outside the box is what enables humans to advance. The imaginative, creative parts of our brain, our right-brains, are where we get out of the box. The right brain is just as necessary and valuable for progress as the left logical brain. The best expression of our humanness is the connection and development of both sides of our brains.

During the past decade, the extraordinary costs of educating our children has been a focus, both nationally and locally. I've watched with dismay as people have voted to cut programs in sports, music, and art. Those cuts are amputating right-brains. The votes are cast in the light of what it costs to fund those programs. What people are not paying attention to is the cost of *not* funding those programs. The taxpayers may be saving dollars, but they are wasting minds.

Recent research has documented the enormous advantage in thinking capacity that children gain when they are taught music as youngsters. Music integrates both sides of our brains and learning music creates physiological connections in the brains of children who learn it. They have more learning capacity. Why are we voting to cut our learning capacity? Obviously, lack of consciousness is not limited to individuals. Millions of people simultaneously can be oblivious.

When my younger son, Alden, was a sophomore in high school, he took a photography elective during the fall semester. I spent some time with him for a couple of afternoons throwing trash cans up in the air for him to photograph mid-flight. A rather bizarre assignment! As we finished decorating the Christmas tree that year he said, "I want to take a picture of the tree." The next thing I knew he was lying on his back underneath the tree shooting the picture up through the branches. Eureka! What he had gained from that elective course was one of the most valuable things he could have learned—change your perspective, don't necessarily look at things head on, see it from a different angle. Increase your consciousness!

In high school Alden also learned how to compute the angles of a triangle. That's a good, practical skill to have. But if I had to choose for him which piece of learning was more valuable and had more potential benefit to his life, I'd bargain for the insight about a flexible perspective. He can always go to a reference and refresh his memory about how to find the angles. Turning things around and viewing them from a different perspective opens up unlimited horizons for him.

Minds are like muscles—if you don't exercise them they get soft, flabby, and atrophy. They lose their capacity and power. To stay in top form mentally, we need to use both sides of our brain, the left, logical side and the right, creative side. As it makes no sense to do bicep curls with just one arm, it also makes no sense to use just one side of our brains. The real capacity, the real power, lies in well-developed, highly conscious, integrated brains.

STAYING IN YOUR RIGHT MIND—PSYCHOLOGICALLY

I ran the Hawaii Ironman Triathlon in 1988. I had a decent swim and got on to the bike course feeling quite good. Within the first half mile of the 112 mile bike ride, I encountered the Pay and Save Hill which is about the same grade as the World Trade Towers. I struggled up over the hill, weaving back and forth across the road to avoid toppling over. I got to the top and headed out onto the highway. I couldn't get settled into a comfortable rhythm. I was struggling and tense. I found myself wondering if someone had dipped my rear wheel into a vat of bubble gum or if my brakes were rubbing against my tires. To make matters worse, other cyclists kept whizzing by me. Whoosh, whoosh, whoosh. My confidence ebbed like the tides in the Bay of Fundy and I started questioning, "Rita, what are you doing here? Whatever made you think you could do this. You don't belong here. Woman, you are out of your class. After all the people here are world-class athletes, some of the best endurance athletes in the world. Whatever made you think you belonged here?" Was I in my right mind? Absolutely not! I was in my **wrong** mind. I wanted to have a good race. Running that string of negative, self-defeating thoughts was definitely being in my wrong mind. It was totally counterproductive.

From somewhere came the sound of my own voice, "Rita!" the voice demanded. "Shut up and keep pedaling! You just get to the next aid station (every five miles there were aid stations where wonderful volunteers passed out water, Coke, sports drinks, cookies, fruit, and encouragement). When you've picked that one off, you just pick off the next one. If you just pick them off one at a time, you'll finish the bike." That was how I completed the bike ride, one aid station at a time. The stern orders from myself put me back into my "right mind."

The ability to shift from your wrong mind to your right mind is an invaluable skill. I use it whenever I find myself getting overwhelmed. At times during the writing of this book, I found myself shifting into my wrong mind. I started questioning whether I had bitten off more than I could chew. The young girl who thought she wasn't bright enough to go to college rose within me and asked, "What makes you think you've got the ability to write a bestseller? You know, there are some 5 *million* manuscripts submitted every year. What chance do you think you've got?" I was in my wrong mind.

My right mind says, "You don't have to worry about that now. The task you need to focus on right now is writing the next few sentences. You may not have a bestseller here, but you have something to say that you passionately believe in and think would benefit others. You certainly won't have a bestseller or even a book unless you keep writing."

When I was doing technical rock climbing I sometimes stood at the bottom of a cliff, looked up and said, "Holy mackerel (figure of speech from a Maine coast childhood!), I can't climb that!!" I soon realized that I was out of my right mind. I did not need to be concerned about what was "up there" and out of sight while I was standing on the ground at the foot of the cliff. What I needed to do was figure out where the first handhold was, then the second, the first foothold, then the second. Then I needed to find where the next handhold was. I learned that a climb was just a sequence of moves and that having made one move gave me a different vantage point from which to plan the next. I always found or created the resources that I needed as I climbed to get to the top of the cliff.

In rock climbing or in life, one's perspective changes as one moves through a problem or challenge. Resources that you cannot see from the ground become obvious as the view changes. One of the ways to stay in your right mind is to believe that you will find or create all the resources that you need to meet any challenge you set out for yourself. As Julia Cameron reminds us, "Leap and the net will appear."

Rock climbing taught me the very valuable skill of binocular vision which is the ability to *keep your eye on the goal, but focus on the task at hand*. If I don't keep my eye on the goal, the drift of events in my life will quite likely distract me from the goals. The busyness and demands of our lives eat up the time very quickly. It is all too easy to spend one's time on the things that are urgent but not important and never get to the things that are important but not urgent.

WATCH WHAT YOU SAY AND THINK.

What you say to yourself, particularly about yourself, is critical in determining the course of your life. Most of us say things to ourselves that we'd sue someone else for saying. At the very least we'd be terribly hurt and angry and terminate our friendships with those who talked to us in such disparaging terms. The people who say negative, derogatory things to us are toxic to us. It doesn't matter who the speaker is—you or someone else. Toxic words are toxic words no matter what the source.

When I was working as a weight loss clinician, women would sometimes come in and say, "I was so bad this week." My impulse was to get up on my desk and yell, "No!, No!, No! You are not bad. Ax murderers and pedophiles are bad. People who overeat chocolate cake are not bad!" That's self-imposed toxicity. It's corrosive and damaging. It's very, very hard to do positive things for yourself when you are saying negative things to yourself. When you drive you don't put one foot on the gas and the other on the brake and expect to make forward progress. Negative thoughts are brakes on your life.

Another thing I frequently hear are comments like, "I'm so fat" or "I always procrastinate" or "I"m so clumsy." No! No! No! That's instant pre-play. Your subconscious mind has no way of distinguishing what you say from objective reality. Your subconscious mind takes the words at face value, as true. When I say I'm fat, I am programming myself to be fat. When I say I'm a procrastinator, I am helping myself procrastinate. When I say I'm clumsy, or stupid, or poor, I'm programming myself to create those conditions in my life. Life is difficult enough without using your mind to create additional obstacles for yourself.

As a triathlete, running was the most difficult area for me to improve. I discovered that I was saying to others and to myself, "I am a slow runner." Why didn't I just tie my running shoes together and try to run that way? How did I expect to improve my run times while telling myself I was a slow runner? When I became conscious of that, I rewrote the program and told myself that I was a fast runner who was getting faster all the time. My run times improved.

Staying in your right mind requires saying only positive things to yourself. *Please note: Your behavior has to be consistent with your thoughts to get the results you want.* I recently observed a woman checking out of a pharmacy. She purchased a *Health* magazine and a package of cigarettes!

How's that for inconsistency? If I tell myself that I am a slender, fit person when I eat several hundred more calories a day than I need, I am not likely to change my dress size. Focusing on what you want is instant preplay for the results you want. Saying negative, hostile things to yourself while trying to achieve positive results is another way to go north and south simultaneously. You'll go nowhere—fast.

A very important consideration about staying in your right mind is the words that you say to yourself. Think about the words "problem or challenge." I'd much rather have a challenge than a problem. Even more, I'd like to have an opportunity. The situation doesn't change at all, but the labeling changes my attitude enormously. Labeling something a problem casts it in a negative light. Calling the same situation an opportunity or a challenge makes it seem more positive and more manageable. Nobody wants a problem. We all want opportunities. The more positively I feel about a situation, the more likely I am to master it. When I say, "I can't," I am actively working against myself. It's the equivalent of rowing forward with one oar and backward with the other. All that does is keep you going in circles.

When the ERA amendment failed, I responded with sadness and told myself that I would be a second-class citizen for the rest of my life. Years later, a friend said women he knows had a different reaction. Their reaction was, "No way. I'm not second-class to anyone." The instant I heard that I stopped being a second class citizen. Changing the way I viewed the situation changed my reality. I will never be second class to anyone again. I used to be uncomfortable and uneasy around people who I perceived to have higher status or power than I. I would hesitate to speak up or express my opinions. I was self-conscious and uneasy around them. In both instances, I was in my "wrong mind." I don't have to wait for external circumstances to change before I change my reality. I simply can get into my "right mind." Life is a lot easier and I no longer miss interacting with some very interesting people because I'm out of my right mind.

Several years ago, I participated in a search committee. The hospital where I worked was interviewing candidates for the chief of psychiatry position. I was the only female and the only middle manager. The other members of the committee were a vice-president and several physicians. The nonverbal language of the group quickly told me that as far as they were concerned, I was non-existent.

At a meeting one day we were discussing a candidate. He had presented with very good credentials and was personable and warm during the interview. He did not, however, maintain good eye contact and his laugh hit me as too hearty. I did not share my concerns with my colleagues on the committee. I knew they weren't really interested in my opinion, and I also knew that they were too data-driven to be place any credibility in my "gut" feelings. I left the meeting with the uncomfortable awareness that I had sold myself out in the court of others' opinions. I hadn't maintained my own sense of integrity.

The man got hired. Everybody on that committee lived to regret the decision. The falsity of the laugh and the lack of eye contact were outward signs of inward immorality and duplicity. The man caused untold damage to the department and the hospital for years afterwards. A friend of mine says, "In this life, you get what you deserve." A couple of years later, this doctor decided that I had to go because I wouldn't fire one of my night nurses without cause, the only "cause" being that he was angry because she had insisted he come in to see a patient who needed to be seen. He succeeded in getting me removed from my job. I deserved it. I hadn't told the truth about him when I had the chance.

Do I think that speaking up would have blocked his being hired? Not for a minute. But at least when he turned out to be such a problem, I could have had the satisfaction of saying, "I told you so." I also would have had the greater satisfaction of maintaining my integrity.

INTUITION IS YOUR RIGHT MIND

Sometimes your "right mind" isn't your mind at all. Sometimes it's your gut. If there is anything that I really wish I had been taught when I was a child, it was to listen to my gut, to respect my intuition. As Western logical thinkers, intuition has been devalued and dismissed as a legitimate form of information. Intuition is a legitimate form of knowing. We shouldn't exclusively make our decisions based on our intuitive thought any more than we should totally disregard inductive and deductive forms of reasoning. Both are legitimate and useful in our decision-making.

When I was in my twenties, my fiancé and I looked at an older but liveable 12 room house on 100 acres of land in a town located on the southern coast of Maine. It was selling for $12,500. My intuition told me that we should buy the property as an investment. It wasn't terribly practical or logical for us to buy it, but my gut was saying,"Buy it! Buy it!, Buy it!" My logical, practical fiancé ran the numbers and decided not to buy it. I thought some about buying it on my own, but at that time would have had a very hard time getting a mortgage as a single woman. Someone else bought the house. My intuition was right on the money! Money was just what I lost. That property increased in value phenomenally during the next few decades.

When you get a gut feeling, pay attention to it. You are actively processing information without being able to name the source. One way of using your gut reactions more effectively is to ask yourself why you are reacting as you are. Explore the issue further. What other factors are influencing you that you can't name? The more information you have about any situation in your life, the more likely you are to stay in your "right mind."

Another way of being out of your right mind is caring too much about what others think of you. Being a slave to others' opinions is a form of self-inflicted slavery. Your life is much too important to allow someone else to be the master. If you are a unique individual—and you are—*no one* is qualified to determine what your life is about, or what is essential to your living your life mission to your satisfaction. Eleanor Roosevelt said, "No one makes you feel inferior without your permission." Actually no one else ever makes you feel anything without your permission. Unless you are being held captive, at some level you are giving permission for your life to be just what it is. And even if you are being held captive, you *can and should* be in control of how you react. Victor Frankl's eloquent writing in *Man's Search for Meaning* demonstrates our godlike capacity for maintaining self-control in uncontrollable situations.

I recently observed a woman who appeared to be in her mid-fifties. She was a good 35 - 50 pounds overweight and was wearing tights and a tunic. Her straight gray hair was cut in a very short mannish style with a 2-inch long tuft growing at the center-back of her head. She had eight gold earrings in her right ear, encircling the ear from the lobe to the top. Some of them were dangling with gemstones flashing in the light. Her left ear was bedecked with six more earrings, all gold but not matching any of the right earrings and with stones of different colors. Her movements were energetic. Her facial expression was animated and her eyes sparkled. She was interacting with a little girl, perhaps a granddaughter.

When I first spotted this woman, my reaction was negative. What was this woman doing at a graduation dressed like that? As I watched her, I came to the conclusion that she really didn't care (nor should she) what I or anyone else thought. Good for her! She was not being a slave to public opinion. As I watched her, I felt more and more drawn to her. She was clearly her own woman. Her manner was engaging and warm. She treated the child with affection and respect. It was a brutally hot evening. She was probably a lot more comfortable physically than the women who were wearing pantyhose. She was also probably a lot more comfortable psychologically than many of the others as well.

Coming to your senses and staying in your right mind will require effort, focus, and attention. You will need to make an investment in them. The rate of return will compound and add vigor, enthusiasm, power, and control to your life. You will create more life in your life.

Action Steps

1. Take a walk in your neighborhood. Pretend that you have just moved into the neighborhood. Notice what you notice.
2. If you must worry (a state of being out of your right mind) schedule it for 10 minutes early in the morning. Use that time only for worry and then refuse to worry for the rest of the day. If things come up that you want to worry about, jot them down and leave them until the next day for your worry appointment.
3. After you discover that your success and happiness does not require you to worry constantly, start to wean yourself from daily worrying by scheduling your worry sessions for every other day. Gradually reduce the frequency of worry sessions from every other day to once per week and then once every two weeks. What you will discover is that you are much happier when you worry less and you'll decide to quit such an unproductive activity.
4. Place three different types of foods on a plate, perhaps a bite of fruit, a taste of a sweet treat, and a piece of vegetable. Put on a blindfold and then eat each item, very slowly and carefully, really allowing yourself to experience what you are eating.

5. Select one bite of a favorite food and take as long to eat it as you possibly can. Notice all the sensations eating it creates and catch as many subtle nuances of flavor as you can.

Points to Ponder

- All worrying about tomorrow does is take the joy out of today.
- Take action today, worry tomorrow—every day.
- Good races and satisfying lives are lived as they unfold, not as they are anticipated.
- The thoughts that you feed your mind are the food that nourishes your life. Feed yourself well.
- Don't spend your time, invest it.

Chapter 6

CREATING A MISSION STATEMENT FOR YOUR LIFE

I WALKED TO THE RACE START in darkness. *As I rounded the turn onto Allii Drive the lights and activities of the Hawaii Ironman Triathlon rushed out to meet me. The lights for the television cameras were dazzling and even at 5 A.M. the street was bustling with the comings and goings of athletes, volunteers, race officials, and spectators. In the trees above me a large chorus of birds conversed vigorously. I smiled as I realized that we were reversing the traditional order of things. Today, the birds were up with the people!*

The pre-race jitters were palpable as we athletes moved around the race start area, greeting friends, talking about the mysteries of the day which was unfolding around us, slathering up with sunscreen and Vaseline, and checking and re-checking our gear. The day we had been focused on, and training for for so long had begun.

An air of festival hung over the scene. Helicopters with cameramen hanging out the doors flew overhead, recording the scene. People milled about eating, drinking Kona coffee, laughing, and talking. I watched quietly as the sun began to color the hillsides opposite me. I stopped and watched a wedding in progress at the race start. The couple exchanged their vows. He continued his preparations for the Hawaii Ironman Triathlon. It seemed to me that they weren't giving either the race or the wedding the singular attention that each event deserved. I wondered about the romance of the wedding night with the groom just wanting to go to sleep. Well, maybe he was more of an athlete than I was giving him credit for!

Now it was almost 7 A.M. We crowded onto the edge of the beach and waited for the starter's gun to go off. I stood, looking out over the course

75

wondering what the day was going to bring. Was I going to be successful? Did I have "the stuff" to finish this race? Was I out of my mind—a 46 year old woman about to swim 2.4 miles, bike 112 miles, and then run a marathon, 26 miles 285 yards?

It made sense that I was here. For years, I had said that I liked a challenge. Well, this certainly was going to be a challenge. Even being here, facing the questions, doubts, and hopes was a challenge. Staying calm and focused in the midst of it all was the immediate challenge. It made sense in another way as well. The mission statement of my life begins with Helen Keller's statement, "Life is either a daring adventure or nothing at all." This certainly was an adventure. Here I was, standing with 1200 other athletes, standing among the best endurance athletes in the world, about to begin the Hawaii Ironman. Wow! Not your typical day in the life of a wife and mother of two. I was a long way from the fat kid in West Bath, Maine.

I remembered the first time I had read Helen Keller's words. They seared themselves into my soul. I felt that she had written those words just for me. I knew that I had found an idea that really spoke to me at the deepest level of my being, just as I heard the words from Auntie Mame, "I want to live!" Although I didn't realize it at the time, those two short phrases were the foundation for the mission statement for my life. They were grounded in the core of my being. They resonated with truth for me. They excited me. They added deeply to my understanding of who I was and how I wanted to live. They had led me here to the shores of Dig Me Beach and the Hawaii Ironman Triathlon.

The starter's gun went off and I ran into the clear warm water of the Pacific, now being churned by 1200 pairs of arms and legs, a human Cuisinart. I lifted off the bottom and began swimming, trying to go as fast as I could, trying to stay focused, relaxed and calm. I was boxed in by other swimmers and couldn't get free to move around them. For much of the swim I was caught in that box. I kept looking for the opportunity to break out and simultaneously decided to just relax and "go with the flow." It certainly wasn't lonely out there!

The water was clear and beautiful, so clear that I could see the bottom some 90 feet below me. During training swims, I had thoroughly enjoyed swimming in the clear water and watching the rainbowed tropical fish swimming below me. This morning I noticed that the fish had left the neighborhood. The onslaught of 1200 swimmers was apparently too much disturbance for them. One hour and seventeen minutes after the gun went off, I emerged from the water, ran up the ramp, and raced to my bicycle.

I was feeling great. Although my swim time was some ten minutes slower than I wanted, I felt good, strong and easy. That lasted for approximately fi mile until I reached the Pay and Save Hill. You already know how I crashed right into a huge hill inside my head. As in the swim, I needed to let go of the frustration of things not being just as I wanted, and let them be as they were. I needed to stay focused and relaxed. I needed to let this be just what it was—a great adventure.

Once I had settled into the strategy of picking off aid stations, the ride went more smoothly. I moved steadily and surely across that long undulating stretch of black highway. I wasn't blasting the course, but I was riding consistently and steadily. At times, I did a little sightseeing, catching glimpses of the Pacific along the Kona coast, but mostly just riding through the moonscape of black lava, hot sun, and the ever-present wind. Just before the turnaround, the halfway point at Hawi, there is a brutally long, unceasing hill. I toiled up it, totally focused now on just keeping the pedals turning. Finally! Reward time! The turnaround! I eased back, relaxed a bit, grabbed fluids from those wonderful volunteers and happily anticipated the next phase of the race. What goes up must come down. Now I had several miles of downtime—downhill time when I could just let it fly. Spinning my legs every so often to keep the blood flowing, I just cruised. There were more tough miles ahead of me, but this section of the race was just about enjoyment and fun.

Six hours and forty-five minutes after I mounted my bike at the pier, I dismounted and handed it off to the volunteers who directed me into the changing tent. My legs were so stiff, I could hardly walk. I hobbled into the change tent and changed into my running shoes. Two down and one to go! Just a marathon left and I could cross the finish line of the Hawaii Ironman Triathlon!

I stood up and eased into a walk, then into a jog. At the very beginning of the run, there was another one of those huge, long, steep, spirit-breaking hills. I slowed to a walk and walked my way to the top, made the turn onto the road, and started to run. The walk had eased the stiffness and I began to run through the afternoon quite easily. The road followed the coastline and I delighted in the views of waves crashing against the shore, the sight and smell of tropical flowers that edged the road, and the encouragement and support of spectators and fellow athletes.

Unlock Your Possibilities

The road led back into town and then I was climbing that awful Pay and Save Hill again. I think I may have run it in less time than it took me to bike up it in the morning! Back out on the Queen Kaahumanu Highway and I settled into the run. For several miles I traveled five to six feet behind two older men from West Germany. They were happily chatting in German while I happily dogged their heels. Focusing on the motion of their feet, I used them as a sort of cruise control. In some way, their energy helped pull me along. Gradually, they began to pull away from me and I was running alone.

Mile after mile passed. I celebrated at each aid station, here only a mile apart. I picked up water and Coke and energy from the aid stations, slowing to a walk so that I could drink. I never did master the art of running and drinking simultaneously. Water in your nostrils is one thing, but Coke is quite another! I walked through the aid stations, then required myself to break back into a run.

My body felt fine. My mind kept urging me to slow down and walk. Whenever I evaluated the idea, I realized that I felt too good physically to walk. I didn't need to walk. I could just keep running. As the miles wore on, the fatigue grew. The walks through the aid stations became longer and longer and after mile twenty I began to walk the uphills.

Day had passed and I was now running in darkness and watching the full moon rise in the sky. It was beautiful and peaceful. After the heat of the day the soft coolness of the night was most welcome. We had calume lightsticks attached to our shorts to make us visible in the darkness. I watched the line of bobbing light sticks moving in front of me, like a human strand of Christmas tree lights.

At last, I turned the corner and ran down the Pay and Save Hill. Excitement began to build. I was home! Just a few more yards now and I would cross the finish line. The side of the road was lined with spectators now and the applause and encouragement was an infusion of energy into my weary body. As I came around the final turn onto Allii Drive, I felt a surge of joy! The television lights, the cheering crowds, the sound of applause! It was like running into fireworks. The fatigue was gone! My body, so reluctant to move in the darkness and solitude of the Queen Kaahumanu Highway, moved with speed, suppleness, and grace. Triumph and joy exploded within me. Grinning, I placed my left foot on the red line and finished the Hawaii Ironman Triathlon.

Completing the Hawaii Ironman Triathlon was an expression of who I am. The experience was deeply connected to my grounding as a physical person who wants to live with passion and excitement. The experience, like the other big adventures of my life, was born out of my understanding of what I wanted my life to be. I didn't always have that understanding. I have created it and evolved it from the time I was a young woman.

I didn't have the advantage of being told as a young woman my life would be richer, fuller, and more meaningful if I had a personal mission statement, if I was determined, as Joseph Campbell says, to "follow my bliss." I now know that setting out to live a life without a plan is like attempting to build a house with little knowledge of structural engineering and no blueprints. You may end up with a liveable structure, but it will only be a matter of luck. You are much more likely to end up with a structure where the roof leaks and the rooms are too small to contain your dreams. Your structure will much more likely match your needs if you determine what it is that you want, create the plan, gather the materials, and then set about building—whether it is a house or your life.

Most people want to have a "good life." You obviously do or you wouldn't be reading this book. Have you thought specifically about what, for you, would create a "good life?" What is meaningful for you may be different from your neighbor across the street.

One of the challenges we face is our awareness of so many options. No longer limited by geography or awareness, we can choose to live in the city, the country, in the nation where we were born or to move to another part of the world. Our job opportunities are practically limitless. If we look in the *Dictionary of Occupational Titles* (a huge book) and don't find a job that suits us, we can create our own.

All the options can be overwhelming. To avoid the discomfort of feeling overwhelmed, we narrow our focus and don't explore the options. When my sons were little, Toys R Us was a store where I sometimes shopped. When I went into that store I struggled to find what I wanted in the midst of all those boxes, colors, and long, long aisles that reached upward, practically beyond the limits of my ability to see.

My tactic for managing the confusion was to have a mission statement for my trips to Toys R Us in the form of a shopping list. Knowing what I wanted made the shopping easier.

Knowing what you want in the shopping trip of life makes that trip easier as well. Having a personal mission statement helps you know which of the multiple myriad of opportunities that life presents will be more pleasing and gratifying when placed in your life's shopping cart.

The choices I made at Toys R Us were based on my values. I wanted toys for my children that were educational. I make a statement of my values when I say that toys and education should not be separated. I wanted toys that would keep my sons physically active—another value. I tried to avoid the "toys" of violence—again my values being expressed in my choices.

Thinking about and formulating my own value code creates the grounding of my mission statements. Knowing who you are or want to be, knowing what values you consider to be essential for the living of your "good life" is the foundation on which to build your life. It provides an anchor, a source of continuity while at the same time allowing freedom of action to meet the challenges of change and growth.

The socialization process of my childhood laid out a life plan, created a mission statement as it were, that was not about my unique individuality. The socialization process started me out on a path that was about conforming to someone else's beliefs about how a young girl growing up on the coast of Maine should live. I was given a religion. The vocational choices I saw as appropriate for me were teacher, nurse, secretary, and wife. That limited menu was imposed by the values of the culture, of the times. I had no knowledge or awareness that there were other things that I could do. I expected that I would marry and have children. I understood that was my destiny as a woman. Indeed, I understood that not to be married was sign of colossal failure on my part. It never occurred to me, nor did anyone suggest, that I could craft and create my own life, based on my values and directed by my desires. No one suggested that I could live by design not by default.

There were some interesting women in my family who might have been role models if I had learned to see them that way. One was my maternal grandmother who died several years before I was born. In my mother's belongings there was a picture of her, taken right after the turn of the twentieth century, as a member of the high school basketball team. Here was my grandmother as an athlete. At that time she was probably pushing out a frontier, being a pioneer. I learned little of her story.

Another woman was my Great Aunt Nan. She was an elderly woman who I saw as fussy and rather pathetic. She was stilted and formal, and I don't recall ever making anything but polite conversation with her. She had never married. I saw that as a big deficit. Only as an adult did I discover that she had been a business woman. She had lived independently in Portland and supported herself. I certainly wish I had learned more about her life. The polite conversations were a lost opportunity to learn about what her life was like, what had been the challenges, the satisfactions, the successes, and the failures. Not ever talking to her about her life was a lost opportunity to explore options.

When I was four, the present I most wanted for Christmas was a milk truck like my Daddy's. To my parent's credit, that's what I got. At four, I wasn't limited in my thinking about what I could do, who I could be. It was later that I learned to "color between the lines." The culture assumed a role of telling me who I could be, who I "should" be. No one ever suggested to me that the roles and goals to which I was aspiring were not the only ones I could consider. No one ever asked me what I loved to do or suggested that my life was uniquely my own, a blank canvas which I could design and color in any way that I chose.

I observe my mother and my Aunt Barbara, two of the strongest, most capable women on the face of the earth. They are both intelligent, well-read, thoughtful, empathic, and insightful. The knowledge and life wisdom those two women possess is profound. Like most people, the circumstances of their lives have kept them from fully utilizing, developing, and expressing their capacity. That is a loss for the quality of their lives, for the pleasure and experiences that they did not have. It is also a loss for the world. I wonder what those women might have created or done if they had been encouraged to unlock their possibilities. Their expression has been through their children, a valid and useful expression. But the singular, unique contributions that only they could have made are unrealized. Their full potential, enormous unique potential, has gone unexpressed.

The vocational choices for young people today are far less limited, particularly for women. With the freedom of choice comes a higher level of responsibility. It's easier to make a choice when the options are as limited as the ones I knew. It's much scarier in today's world where the message is "you are all self-employed." Wow! That puts me out there! Another daunting part of today's message is that I can't just learn a profession—preferably a well-paying one—and live comfortably ever after. Today's message is that I have to keep learning and mastering new skills for the rest of my life—just to stay current.

The array of choices is bewildering. Just as it is much easier to decide what to have for dinner when there are only two or three things on the menu than it is at a smorgasbord, so it is when perusing the menu of life choices. The wide range of choice can itself be intimidating. Because I don't like the discomfort of not knowing where my path lies, there is a temptation to make a quick, not fully considered choice.

A personal mission statement is a valuable asset for staying focused on your direction, for living a life according to your values, not the ones you've been told you should have, but the ones that by your own assessment are the values that you want to live by, the ones that are in harmony with your deepest desires. Without being connected to and living those desires, you will not really live. Without that connection to and expression of who you are, life is reduced to existence.

In the course of living in the ocean of life all of us get buffeted by the winds and currents. It is very easy to get dragged by the current into a place we don't wish to be. If I have a mission statement and life blows me off course, I can simply re-focus on my mission statement and move back onto the course. Without a mission statement, I am subject to just drifting through life, going wherever the currents move me.

We currently live in a culture that suggests it is possible for us to "have it all." The reality is we can't have it all. We are limited by time, so choosing one thing means that we are not choosing others. The trick is to be very careful about what you pick. What you choose has to be done in accordance with what it is that your heart really desires. I have a yellowed page from an old calendar on my bulletin board. On it there is a message from Katherine Whitehorn: "Find out what you like doing best and find someone to pay you for doing it." She's right on the money! The process of creating your mission statement is a means of helping you sort out what it is that you most want to do. Given that your time is limited and you can't do it all, have it all, what will be most satisfying and gratifying?

Our culture says that Whitehorn's idea is impractical. We are taught that first you have to have a job—the work you do to earn money. After your job is done and you have met your other responsibilities, the remaining time is yours to do what you want. Wrong! Wrong! Wrong! We are much better served when we do what we love and let the avenue for earning money open up through that channel. Can you imagine how our world would be transformed if everyone did work they loved and found meaningful? Given that that is probably not going to happen soon, why not transform your own world and decide that you are going to live your life doing what you love?

Some of us are very disconnected from our heart's desires. We don't have a clue as to what it is that we really want. Recently I led a weekend workshop and asked the participants to outline the activities that they would do on a perfect day. One woman ended up in tears because she couldn't think of what she would do. She was a successful, accomplished business woman who was so constrained by doing what others expected that she couldn't even think of what it was the she'd like to do.

The good news about her situation is that once she had allowed herself to see what her situation was, once she got out of the denial, she was in a position to deliberate about what is was that she really wanted. Coming out of denial is inevitably a painful process, but the alternative is staying unaware and never allowing your heart's desires to be realized. Allowing herself to come out of the denial was her ticket to getting free.

Another woman who attended one of my workshops was a lawyer who no longer wanted to practice law. She felt constrained by concerns about how her family and friends would react if she quit and opened up a health-food store. She had concerns about how she would manage financially. Shortly after the workshop she closed her law practice and is now happily running her business. She is following her bliss and has improved the quality of her life enormously.

VALUES-BASED LIVING

The Declaration of Independence speaks of our "right to life, liberty, and the pursuit of happiness." The Pledge of Allegiance asserts that this country's values include "equality and justice for all." Those values are core and key to the level of freedom and achievement that the people of the United States have enjoyed for a long time. Those expressed values are a core factor in the success of this democracy. Even though we do not fully live up to the standards of those expressed values, they work better than other values that the founding fathers might have chosen. The evidence is that the founding fathers chose well.

Those values were freely chosen, although not without much arduous soul-searching and discussion. To be able to assert those values, the people of this country paid a very high price in the form of the Revolutionary War. The same is true of individuals. Our values must be freely chosen. There is often a high price to be paid when the people around us are not in agreement with the values we have chosen. Usually the disagreement is not with the values. Virtually everyone would say they believe "honesty is the best policy." Where the interpersonal trouble starts is when we start to live in total commitment to the value of honesty. The husband who says to his wife, "I know that you are drinking almost every day. I believe that you are an alcoholic," will probably not find her being glad that he has spoken the truth.

The ability to choose our own values is paramount. To the extent that we avoid the soul-searching and decision-making about our values, we are living life in someone else's shoes. Mortimer J. Adler writes in *Six Great Ideas*, "With this innate power of free choice, each human being is able to change his own character by deciding for himself what he shall do or shall become. *We are free to make of ourselves whatever we choose to be (italics mine).*"

The quality of your life depends on the quality of the values that you choose—and hold yourself accountable for living up to. It is important to know what your own personal values are (as distinct from those you grew up being told you should believe in) and to live by them. When we violate those values, we know it. If we defend ourselves by denial, we still carry the burden of that violation. If we profess to believe in honesty and then tell a white lie, we are violating our own standard.

One of the burdens of this culture is the double standard about truth. We are taught that honesty is a value and also that we should "make nice" and not hurt anyone's feelings. As children we are instructed to be honest and then told not to tell Grandma about Daddy's drinking because it would upset her. The child who screams, "I hate you, Mommy!" and is told "Don't say that! You don't hate Mommy" is being taught to be dishonest. At the moment of the statement, the child's true emotion is hate. Being told she doesn't feel that way by the powerful, all-knowing mother-god person makes her distrust her own perceptions. Being told not to say what she thinks is a direct lesson in being dishonest. The four year old who makes a statement about how fat Mrs. Jones is gets quickly shushed up. He knows that the reality is that Mrs. Jones is fat, that her fatness is a truth. Shushing him up tells him that there are negative consequences about telling the truth. The ultimate lesson taught is—don't always tell the truth. One can't be partially honest anymore than one can be partially pregnant. It's either/or.

The four-year old might better be coached in understanding that words can be weapons and can inflict pain that is even more hurtful than knives or stones. He needs to know that, yes, it is true that Mrs. Jones is fat and that he has no right or obligation to give her feedback without her asking his opinion. He needs to know that what Mrs. Jones chooses to do with her body is her concern, and her concern only, and that to render unsolicited opinion is an intrusive act on his part. He also needs to know that it is not okay to unnecessarily cause pain to another person and that calling Mrs. Jones fat is likely to cause her pain.

Years later, that child as an adult may be asked by his wife, "Honey, do you think I'm too fat?" Even if his wife is 100 pounds overweight, he is apt to say, "No," because he doesn't want to cause an argument or to hurt her feelings. He may think that he is sparing her feelings, but suppose that he really does think she's too fat and doesn't find her sexually desirable as a result. The end result of his white lie? He's not told the truth and she knows it. Now she not only recognizes that he thinks she's too fat but that the relationship isn't strong enough to stand up to the truth. She'll leave the conversation feeling alienated, not supported as she wanted. He'll leave the conversation feeling alienated as well. His relationship with his wife is laid on a shallow, inauthentic base. Authentic relationships require total honesty.

If I keep a secret from you, if I have places in my mind that are labeled "off limits" to you, then that part of me is inaccessible to you. We cannot be in a relationship in those off limits areas. The more parts of me I place off limits, the less of me is available to you. The husband loses in the authenticity of his relationship to his wife by his "white lie," he also loses in his relationship to himself because he knows that he was dishonest. Most of us arrive at some semblance of adulthood by our early twenties. What we have learned is how to assume the roles and posturing of adults. It is a rare person who feels free to truly express herself. Most of us have places within ourselves where we feel ashamed of ourselves.

When I was twenty-one never on God's earth would I have told anyone that I was a bedwetter until I was thirteen. I was so ashamed and humiliated by that. I wouldn't have told you how uncertain I was about my sexuality. I wouldn't have told you how uneasy I was because I wasn't in a relationship destined for marriage. I wouldn't have been honest with you about how much it hurt to see myself as fat. I was so good at presenting confidence that a nursing school classmate's husband told me years later that he had always wanted to ask me out but never had because I was so confident. Isn't that a hoot? The defense I put on to keep my hurt from showing about my lack of success with men kept at least one from approaching me. I wish I thought that I was born and reared in some backward time and that those things are no longer happening. I think they still happen. We humans preen and posture and "play the role" to protect our egos. We end up feeling alienated and alone because nobody really understands us.

If we don't relate to others on the basis of total truth, we cannot be in a genuine relationship with them. We know they are relating to the role person we are presenting ourselves to be, not the real person we are. The fear we live with is that if they really knew who we were, they wouldn't want to stay with us. They, in the meantime, are probably in their own partially hidden role mode and have the same concerns. It certainly is difficult to live "happily ever after" if, at some level, there's a fear that some day he (she) will find out who I really am—and probably leave me.

The lobsters on the coast of Maine where I grew up shed their shells annually. Without shedding, they cannot grow. When the old hard shell is removed, they are covered with a softer, leathery skin. While they are "soft-shelled" they are vulnerable to predators. Humans are the same way with their roles. The roles I assume are the hard, protective coverings that I use to keep me psychologically safe. They are also restricting, confining. They stunt my growth. In order to grow, I need to shed my old shell and be willing to tolerate feeling vulnerable. In order to be in an authentic relationship, I need to shed my roles and be honest.

Brad Blanton in *Radical Honesty* says "Roles are like clothing we put on to protect ourselves from the cold. When we take off the roles we have been hiding behind, the naked being we are stands there—vulnerable and defenseless. The *being* we are, as distinct from the roles we've been playing, doesn't need the defensive weapons we invented to scare the enemy away."

The ironic and sad part of the roles is that while they may help us survive, they don't help us *live*. Indeed, they suck the life right out of us. The more we buy into the roles, the less authentic life we live. The words "boss," "mother," "father," "sister," "doctor," and "secretary," all have standardized expectations, "shoulds" built into them. The more I deal with others from the stance of those role definitions, the less of the real me, the living, thinking, throbbingly alive "me" is available to them. The role of Ralph de Bricassart in *The Thornbirds* is instructive. He lived his entire life in the role of successful Catholic priest. A vital part of him was deeply in love with Meggie. He lived his entire life in denial of himself. When he sat in the garden and realized that he had made the wrong choice all those years, the knowledge killed him. The reality was he had been killing himself gradually for his entire adult life.

HEALTH

Most of us would say we value health. Indeed there is a widespread recognition that if you don't have good health, whatever else you have diminished in value. With that widespread knowledge, why is one third of the adult population obese? There is no doubt that obesity causes all sorts of harm to the human body. Heart disease, diabetes, and cancer all occur more often in obese people. The last time I looked all those diseases were a great source of pain and distress. Why do we behave in ways that are contradictory to our best interests?

With widespread knowledge of the value of health, why do one quarter of us still smoke? Why are affluent, young people smoking cigars? There is little doubt that regular exercise confers great health benefits. Why do less than half of the population engage in a regular exercise habit? Why do we behave in ways that are contradictory to our best interests?

People are wary of the pesticides that get put into our food supply because of fears of cancer. A much higher percentage of cancer can be traced to the types of foods that we put into our mouths, the high fat, high sugar stuff that Americans consume by the ton. The high fat, high sugar stuff fills us up and is devoid of the vitamins and minerals that we need. According to the Tufts University *Health & Nutrition Letter* (June 1997, Vol. 15, No. 4) fewer than half of us eat the three or more servings of vegetables per day that are recommended.

One factor is denial. As an acquaintance said to me recently; he didn't exercise, he had a friend "who had gone running and died." Jim Fixx died in the 1970s and people still use him as an example of how running is bad for you. Running, or any other kind of exercise, does not create immortality. And yes, there are people who die of heart attacks while running. However, the most common time for heart attacks is 9 A.M. on Monday morning. I've never heard anyone say they weren't going to work on Monday morning because they might have a heart attack!

NOT CAUSING UNNECESSARY PAIN

Not ever causing unnecessary pain to another is a good sound value. If all of us adhered to that standard this world would be transformed. If it is good policy to not cause pain to others, doesn't it make sense that we shouldn't cause unnecessary pain to ourselves either? Don't we deserve at least the same level of respect and consideration that others are due?

As a culture we are making the wrong choice with regard to our health. We are indulging our passions for French fries, Ben and Jerry's, and the remote control switch at the expense of our real good—our health.

PERSONAL MISSION STATEMENT

The personal mission statement that guides my life is "My life is to be an adventure. In the course of that adventure, I plan to learn as much as I can and to develop myself as much as possible, physically, intellectually, emotionally, and spiritually. I also want to share as much as I can with as many people as I can."

I have found it to be a good guideline for my life. One week before I moved out of the marital home where I had the benefit of a shared six-figure income, I learned that the company for whom I did seminars was not going to be doing them any more. Fifty thousand dollars of anticipated income flew out the window in one phone call. Given the poverty of my childhood, that was primal terror. I remember saying to myself, "Wow! This is scary. Maybe you'd better stay." Within seconds I asked myself, "Rita, what is your life about? Remember your mission statement?" I knew the answer. I thought, "There's a name for women like that, and you're not one of them. You go." I went. A woman of adventure would not stay in an unhappy marriage for the security of an income.

Later, as I struggled with the trials and challenges of being an entrepreneur, the security of a nursing job tempted me. Being aware of my mission statement made it easier to remain committed to my goals and more importantly, staying true to the person I have declared myself to be. In both those situations, I made my decisions based on my values. They were the right decisions for my life.

Action Steps

1. Write your own obituary. What do you want to be remembered for? Your obituary will help you clarify what's important to you.
2. Design your perfect day. On a sheet of paper write down the things you would do or experience on a "perfect day." Are the activities of your life providing you with any of those experiences?
3. Give yourself your "perfect day." Sometime in the next two weeks, plan a day where you do as many of the activities from your perfect day as you can.
4. If time and money were of no concern, what would you do? On paper, answer the question.
5. Think about the happiest times of your life and journal about them. Set the writing aside for several days, then re-read what you wrote. As you read, ask yourself what the common threads are and what made those experiences so satisfying.

Points to Ponder

- You never lose out when you maintain your integrity. You never win when you don't.
- Follow your bliss and doors will open for you where there were no doors before. — Joseph Campbell
- When you keep a secret from someone, you diminish intimacy and connection.
- Too many secrets build uncrossable chasms.
- Happiness is a choice.

Chapter 7

LEARNING TO LIVE IN THE SKINNY BRANCHES

I STOOD AT MY CAMPSITE *on the coast of Maine watching the sun's final rays dance across the water. I was talking with my sister, Sally, and telling her about my plan to leave my secure hospital job and earn my living as a speaker. As a newly divorced woman, income concerns were a necessary reality to confront. I knew that my heart lay with the speaking, and I knew that it is not easy to start a business from scratch. I didn't have much capital; I didn't have an office or equipment, I didn't have a clientele. But I was charged up and turned on by the speaking. I saw speaking as a means of living and the hospital job as merely a means of support. As a woman in my early fifties, I had a sense that if I was going to follow my bliss into speaking, I needed to do it soon.*

Sally's comment was, as she listened to me, "Wow! You really are living out there in the skinny branches." I had never heard the comment before and was intrigued by it. She had learned it in a personal growth seminar several years before. I liked the term "skinny branches" and thought a lot about the metaphor.

Among the conclusions that I came to is that living in the skinny branches is where the real living is. When you are out in the skinny branches, you get to see the view, you get to see the sunrise and the sunset, feel the wind and the rain. You get to know the moon and the stars. You experience the storm and may even spend some hairy moments hanging on and hoping you've got the strength to make it. While you are doing so, you are gaining strength and skill at being able to manage both the storm and yourself. The branches are also where the fruit is.

The alternative is to live in close to the trunk, ostensibly a safer place.

Unlock Your Possibilities

The trunk is scratchy and hard. You'll still get wet when it rains. You may not blow around in the storm quite as much, but you'll still experience the storms. You won't have the view or the joy of soaring as the breeze blows the branches. You'll miss learning the skills of riding the branches. And—someone still may show up with a chain saw and buzz your tree down.

The truth is, if you are alive—ALL THE BRANCHES ARE SKINNY.

Later, I told a friend about the conversation. He told me that in the West, the traditional story is of the boy being warned that if he goes up in the high thin branches he will fall. Disregarding the advice of the elders, he climbs and as predicted by the elders, falls and is destroyed. In the East, my friend said, the tradition is that the boy learns to climb in the skinny branches. As he climbs, he gains in competency and skill and learns to master the art of the skinny branches. These two versions of the myth very nicely illustrate that what you expect is what you get.

There is no safety. There is no security. Life is a terminal illness. As Helen Keller observed, "Security does not exist in nature, nor do the children of men as a whole experience it. Avoiding danger is no safer in the long run than exposure." Given that reality, it only makes sense to choose to live in the skinny branches. We are already there.

One of the legacies of our socialization as children is to be more or less comfortable with living in the skinny branches. If we were lucky enough to be socialized in a family where our parents were relatively comfortable with the insecurities of life, then we are apt to be more comfortable with ourselves in taking risks. If our socialization was about being safe, never getting dirty and being too concerned with what other people were thinking about us, then it is likely that our own comfort zone is relatively small and rigid and the idea of living in the skinny branches absolutely terrifies us.

Not too long ago I worked with a social worker who lived about thirty miles outside of Boston. This woman was a few years younger than I and had a Master's degree. She was afraid to drive in the city of Boston. How limiting! I couldn't imagine how she managed to live a life without having the freedom of going into the city whenever she wanted. I have known other women who wouldn't drive after dark. I'm not talking about elderly women with failing eyesight. I'm talking about much younger women whose main visual deficit was in the way they choose to view themselves and their level of competence. Women do not, of course, own the franchise on limiting themselves by their beliefs and unwillingness to move outside their comfort zones. Men who are uneasy and afraid to express emotion or who can't figure out how to put a meal on the table are also limiting themselves.

When you were two you were probably not terrified by the challenges of the world. You were enthralled, delighted, amused, and excited about discovering all you could about the world. Everything fascinated you. You were probably outraged when adults tried to thwart your explorations. If you have ever observed a two-year old you know how persistent they can be in evading or avoiding adult restrictions on their explorations.

I am not, of course, ignoring the fact that there are real dangers in the world that people need to teach their two-year olds to avoid. The child doesn't have the judgment to understand the dangers of sharp knives or safety pins stuffed into electric outlets. Certainly as adults we need to be able to discriminate real dangers from the ones that simply restrict our comfort zones and limit our options. Two-year olds don't know or respect the real limits; too many adults don't know or respect the real possibilities. There is a wide range of experiences, learning, and delight that is well within the zone of reasonable safety and outside your comfort zone of today.

As children, many of us learned to put a fence around what we would allow ourselves to try. To avoid the displeasure and punishment of adults, we learned to take our wants and wishes underground. We learned to distrust what it was that we wanted and to look to others to give us the guidelines. We learned to "play it safe." As a result we stopped playing and life became less free and joyful. If we want a life of freedom and growth and joy, we need to enlarge our comfort zones so that they are wide enough to accommodate the dreams and goals that express our highest potential.

I remember being in first grade and struggling vainly to "color between the lines." I remember looking at Nancy Malone's neatly done, precisely colored picture (as a matter of fact, I remember her neatly curled, magazine perfect blonde hair and seeing it as so much more beautiful than my own unruly mop of curls) and wishing that I could make mine as perfect as hers.

Unlock Your Possibilities

When I was growing up I wish someone could have helped me understand that being able to color between the lines did not determine my value as a person. I wish someone had helped me understand that all of us are unique, with a rich blend of talents, skills, proclivities, and interested and that we are all wonderful. I wish someone had taught me that being able to color outside the lines of our thinking is the basis for creativity and is to be cherished.

The complexity of the contemporary world requires large comfort zones. Because knowledge is growing at exponential rates, the behaviors and attitudes that worked in yesterday's world don't work very well today and will be totally obsolete by tomorrow. The future belongs to the flexible.

I am writing this book on a computer. Today I am very comfortable using the functions that I am familiar with. There are still lots of functions that this computer could do for me if I learned how to use them. It has taken time, effort, and frustration to learn how to use this marvelous tool. There is undoubtedly more time, effort, and frustration ahead of me as computers change and become even more functional, but I could not function very effectively in today's world without being able to use my computer. I will not function in tomorrow's world unless I am willing to keep learning.

I remember vividly one of my early computer encounters. I was taking a research course for my Master's degree. I had to go to the computer lab and run a set of simple statistics. I was somewhat intimidated by the prospect as I went to the lab, but found an open computer, took out my directions, and started to follow them. After fifteen minutes of trying unsuccessfully to log on, I was chagrined and frustrated. Here I was a Master's student and I couldn't even log onto the computer! I started to feel really stupid—not a feeling state that I really like. There were student-tutors available for help, so I appealed to one of them. He gave me more directions. Directions which did not open up the file. I still couldn't log on! I went back for more directions. That still didn't help. Several trips and much frustration and time later, I was no closer to completing my assignment than when I started. After an hour, I quit and left the lab, assignment undone.

During class later that week, I learned what I had been doing wrong. I also discovered that I had not been the only one that had had the same problem. The next time I went to the lab, I successfully logged on and completed the assignment. When I arrived at the lab I was outside my comfort zone. Whenever we do anything new, most of us are outside our comfort zones. It comes with the territory. There is no way to master something new, whether it is a belief, a skill, a job, or a role without being in that place of uneasiness. You have to leave the old place of certainty in order to move to a new place. That famous philosopher Yogi Berra said, "You can't steal second with your foot still on first." One of the difficulties that we humans have is that although we want, really, really want to get onto second base, we hate taking our foot off first.

Whether we like it or not, we are all pioneers. The world is changing, rapidly. There has never been a human experience like the one that is being created today. The knowledge explosion puts us all in a pioneering mode irrespective of whether we want to be there or not. Our only choice lies in deciding whether we are going to adapt or resist. We can go cheerfully and expectantly with the attitude of a two-year old, or we can go reluctantly, but we are going to go. The world is irrevocably different now.

Why are we so reluctant to change? Why do we adapt so slowly? I think it is because we are so reluctant to go into a psychological place where we have to acknowledge that we don't know all the answers, that we are uncertain, that we don't know. That's where we feel like Linus without our blanket or Popeye without his spinach. We hate being the lobster in the soft, vulnerable shell.

The uneasiness with change is nothing new. Throughout history, the proponents of change have met with resistance. Martin Luther, Galileo, Abraham Lincoln, Elizabeth Cady Stanton, and Jocelyn Elders would all tell you that John and Jane Doe do get excited about change, but it is not their rush to change that generates the excitement. I can imagine the prehistoric scene when Malana (why are prehistoric humans always named Urg or something like that?) came racing back to the encampment, all fired up because she had found a warm, dry cave that she thought would make a much more comfortable place to sleep than in the trees where her group slept. Can you hear the conversation as Malana tells them about what she's found? "Listen, this cave would make a great place to sleep. When it rained, we wouldn't get wet. We could have a fire right in the cave. When it was cold, we could sleep near the fire. It would be so great! And we wouldn't have to worry about the little ones falling out of the trees!"

Do you think the group said, "Hey! You're right. What a great idea! Let's go!" I doubt it! I suspect that Malana heard comments like, "Are you crazy? That's not where we sleep. We're humans. Humans sleep in trees. Humans have always slept in the trees."

I won't belabor the point, but Malana and her compatriots lived in an era of very slow change. Hardly anything changed from generation to generation. Now we live in an environment where hardly anything stays the same from one decade to the next. Your ability to thrive in the 21st century will depend on your ability to live in a wide comfort zone, to be comfortable with massive change, and to easily say, "I don't know."

When I was in my early thirties, I thought about how difficult it was for me to acknowledge that I didn't know something. Why did I have the feeling that I *should* know anything, no matter what was being talked about? I realized that I wouldn't expect myself to know about nuclear physics. Why was I expecting myself to know about other things? After all, I couldn't possibly know everything. No one does. Since that time I have given myself permission not to know and permission to ask. No one, not one person, has ever looked at me, aghast and said, "Wow! You really are stupid. In fact, you're too stupid to get it, so I'm not going to tell you."

What I have discovered is the virtually everybody loves to be an expert. They love to tell you about things they know, especially if they are excited about or by the things they know. One way to automatically expand your comfort zone is to decide you are very comfortable acknowledging the things you don't know. It's so much easier than trying to wing it and pretend you know.

CHANGE YOUR MIND OR CHANGE YOUR BEHAVIOR!

When I was studying for my master's degree in counseling, I would occasionally get involved in the coffee shop debate: Was it better to facilitate change by helping people change their minds or change their behavior? Both sides had fervent proponents (and try to change their minds!). My attitude was—and is—why choose? Both are avenues for facilitating change. If you want to change quickly—and you must—use both.

THE MIND AS A BASIS FOR CHANGE

At one time, I leaned more heavily toward the "change the behavior" side of the argument. Now, I tend to be more on the side of "change the beliefs" because I have a deeper appreciation of how potent our beliefs are in keeping us locked in and blocked out of the things that we want. As a puppy my St. Bernard, Serendipity, was taught that the living room was off limits (secondary to my not being a big fan of dog hairs on the couch). One Christmas, when she was all decked out in a big red bow, we decided that we wanted to take her picture sitting beside the Christmas tree. We tried and tried to get her to join us in the living room. Her conflict was visible. Multiple times she started to move forward and then moved back. She obviously wanted to please us. We tried for a long time to get the picture, but she could not violate the deeply engraved behavior. Humans, too, can get restricted by standards that are outmoded and no longer functional.

When I was competing in triathlons, I annually did a race in my hometown. My mother told me about a neighbor who had said to her, "Rita's quite an athlete!" My reaction when I heard the comment was to qualify it, to add "...for a woman her age." I caught myself. "Rita, why did you need to minimize your accomplishment?" The answer was my belief system about myself wasn't big enough to just let the statement stand on its own. As I thought about it, I realized that I wanted to enlarge the scope of my comfort zone to include "quite an athlete," period. The shift I made in my mind was gradual. It took repeated practice before I could acknowledge that I was quite an athlete and not feel a little like an imposter as I said it. Maya Angelou states it best in *I Know Why the Caged Bird Sings* when she says, "I soon found that my new assurance wasn't large enough to fill the gap left by my old uneasiness." It takes time for us to adjust to a new sized self-image.

When I worked in a weight loss clinic, I got another glimpse of how terribly powerful our beliefs are. When the weight loss phase was complete, many, many women had trouble maintaining the loss. There are many reasons, both physiological and psychological for this. One of them is that if a woman lost 50 - 75 pounds, the image that she had in her head about how she looked was different from the one that looked back at her from the mirror. The image in her head, the "fat me," is the "normal" image. That is what she believes that she should look like. The newer, thin image is abnormal, the "imposter me." This creates what psychologists call "cognitive dissonance," two contradictory beliefs. That is a situation that humans don't like! There are two ways for the woman to resolve this dilemma. One is to change the belief in her head. The other is to change the body. Of course, regaining the weight is the quickest, fastest way to resolve the dilemma. Once the weight was regained, the internal image and the external image were consistent. She was fat again, but it felt more "normal" than being thinner.

Alyce Cornyn-Selby, a writer and speaker, has one of the best ways of framing the power of our beliefs that I have ever found. Even better, she's developed a technique to get us past the obstacles they present. Alyce's framing is that we all have some 200 or so characters that live in our heads. We have mother, father, teachers, siblings, significant others, religious instructors, and even famous people living inside our heads. Each of those characters may have an objection to a decision that we are making. Alyce uses the example of finding a classic white car. As you stand in the showroom looking at the car, you think, "Wow! Is that beautiful! I'd look so cool in it." According to Alyce, that's your PR (public relations) director. Another voice says, "But it's white. White gets so dirty." You know who that is—that's Internal Mom. Then another voice chimes in with, "It's too expensive." That's the FD (financial director).

According to Alyce, if you say you want something and then go about making sure you don't get it, that's self-sabotage. Examples: procrastination and yo-yo dieting. That means someone inside you *wants* it but someone else inside you *doesn't* want it. Inside your mind there is someone(s) who objects to your getting what you wnat or someone who thinks things should stay the way they are. Alyce has a technique that she calls the Inner Theatre Method (detailed in the book *The Procrastinator's Success Kit*). You simply dialogue with the person in your head who has objections to your goal. Using writing, you ask to talk with the person who objects. By negotiating with the objecting voice, you can come to a peaceful settlement and create what you want in your life. Alyce says she dialogues for fifteen minues. One fifteen minute dialogue got her the freedom she needed to lose over a hundred pounds and keep it off for some fifteen years now.

I recently had a revelation of my own about how powerful the beliefs that bind us really are. As I've previously indicated, I grew up in very limited financial circumstances (read, poor!). Years ago, I came across an exercise that Tony Robbins recommended to get clearer on internal attitudes towards money. The exercise was to write down everything you'd heard about money when you were a child (I suggest you do this). I started with the cliches—"a penny saved is a penny earned" and the like. I got to the real stuff when I remembered all the times I'd heard my mother say, "We can't afford it." And then, I recalled her saying, "She's very nice for someone who has money." People who have money aren't nice. Wow, that's a framework that will create a conflict around money, won't it?

As I continued the exercise, I realized that I was married to a man who also frequently said, "We can't afford it." It's not surprising that I chose to marry someone with that belief. It mirrored my own childhood experience and, therefore, was very familiar and homey, even though not being able to afford it wasn't what I consciously wanted.

Ambivalence about money is widespread. Perhaps it's because we believe there is a link between our worth as human being and our net worth. Having money becomes a way of keeping score. If I haven't scored high enough on the money scoreboard, I end up feeling ashamed. If you feel that way, please disconnect those thoughts. Stop keeping score (there will always be someone with more money than you, so it's a game you can't win). It makes no sense to play it.

Most people are more open to talking about their sex lives than about their financial lives. Have you had frank conversations about money and how you feel about it with your children or your siblings? If you are not open with close intimates, it's not surprising. Our culture has a taboo about money-talk. If you don't have all the money you want, perhaps there is some ambivalence woven into your belief system that is blockading you from getting the money you want.

As I have continued the introspective work about the impact our families of origin have on our core beliefs, I realized that the theme of my family of origin is "noble suffering." That's a good news/bad news realization. The good news is that the noble part of the theme imparts values that I consider to be important for the living of a good life, honesty, commitment, caring, understanding, striving for excellence. The bad news part of the theme is the suffering bit. The theme of suffering on earth is prominent in the Judeo-Christian beliefs on which our culture is constructed. I am not denying that suffering, sickness, death, and disability are all part of our experience. But I wonder if we make it worse by our expectations. I don't want to live a life of "first you suffer, then you die." Only a cranky, mean God would design a world that worked that way.

We seem to expect to get bad things delivered into our lives. I stop in at the local community store to pick up my mail and I overhear conversations about the weather. Someone will say, "What a fantastic day outside!" Then I hear the response, "Yes, but we'll pay for it later." Why ruin the beautiful day that is today with predictions of gloom and doom for later on? Really, what would happen if we thought life was good and going to get better? In spite of the culture in which I live and the family theme I inherited, I have decided to break away from suffering. I choose "freedom, growth, and joy" as my personal theme.

As I thought about family themes, it seems that there are a number of them. I know of families where the theme is "success at all costs" and others where it's "failure at all costs." Another theme I isolated was that of "angry entitlement." The subtitle of that one is "the world owes me a living—actually a good one, damnit." This is a very popular theme in the United States today. The theme of alcohol and drug users is "it's just too difficult to bear, so I'm getting out of here." I'm sure there are other themes, both constructive and destructive.

In addition to the family themes, there are the individual roles that get assigned to us as children. I was the mature, responsible one, not an unusual assignment for the oldest daughter in a large family. It was certainly a better one than the "family failure" which is a role that some people get assigned early in life.

The themes and roles become strings around our lives. They are powerful predictors of how we will conduct ourselves. It's just fine if the ones that you got were positive and functional. But if, like most of us, there are aspects of your family theme and your roles that hold you back from seeking your dreams, that sap your energy and cause you to sell yourself short, then it's time to declare independence from them and create your own. That will probably take you out of your comfort zone. And that's a basic choice—comfort or freedom. We don't get to have it both ways.

It takes time, effort, and focus to change those basic, core beliefs.

The very first step is to become aware of what the underlying, unconscious beliefs are. In order to get free of them, you have to take the courageous step and examine them. You will also need to confront the reality that others around you may not approve of either your choice to understand the dynamics or to change them. It's one more place where you will need to move out of your comfort zone. If there is something that you decide is important to you that significant others do not approve of and you "go along to get along," you are choosing to live life in someone else's shoes.

I liken the process of changing your beliefs to that of dental braces. First, you make the assessment that the change is needed, then you decide how the teeth should look. You put the braces on, usually the hardest part. Then gradually, over time, you keep increasing the pressure and guiding the teeth—or the thoughts—into place. Given enough time and focus, the teeth and thoughts will maintain themselves without any more outside support from you. The change is permanent.

BEHAVIOR AS THE BASIS FOR CHANGE

The avenue of changing your behavior and causing subsequent changes in beliefs is an equally legitimate means of shaping your life the way you want it to be. On my bulletin board there is a Nike bumper sticker which reads, "Just do it." Those words talk to me about the utility of taking action. When I was rock-climbing, I learned an expression, "Commit to it and go." Climbers, about to make a move that is scary or intimidating, will sometimes think for a long time about making the move. "Commit to it and go" is for me a wonderful reminder that if I've decided to do something, there's not sense hanging around waiting. I might just as well go for it.

I have found that the most difficult step in the process of doing anything is overcoming the inertia and getting into motion. Once I have embarked upon a task or activity, the hardest part is done. That is true whether it is getting out of bed for my morning run, starting the dishes, or writing a dissertation. If I am thinking, "Oh, this bed is so warm and cozy, I really just want to stay here for another half hour," I usually tell myself that I don't have to run far or fast and that if after the first mile I want to quit, I can quit. That ease about the run means I get up, put on my shoes and go out and "do it." I have been running for over twenty-five years. In all that time, there have been approximately three runs that I didn't enjoy. Does that mean it's easy? No. It does require discipline and purpose, but I always, always enjoy the process and love the vital, energetic feeling I have when I'm done.

Years ago when I finished running I would sometimes ask myself, "Are you going to have to do this for the rest of your life?" My answer then was, "Hey, look, you did it today. You don't have to be concerned about tomorrow right now, let alone about forty-five years from now." Now the thought that I have is, "Boy! I sure hope I can do that every day for the rest of my life!"

The mind games I use to get myself to act in my own best interest help me over-come the inertia. I use rewards for myself. There are times when I have made myself Advent calendars of a Christmas tree that I get to put a star on each day during the holiday season when I meet my eating and exercise goals (like most of you, I find the "great All-American eating season" between Thanksgiving and New Year's a challenge). When it's a writing task that I need to get to, I put on a tape or CD and tell myself that I only have to work until the music stops. As with the running, once I'm in motion it's no problem to keep going.

While I was competing in triathlons, my training routine required that I ride a wind trainer (indoor cycling) during the winter. I found it colossally boring. It was *the* most difficult activity for me to get done. So, I invented Pavarotti intervals. I love Luciano's voice, he can sing to me anytime. The deal I cut with myself was that I only had to do one side of a tape. I'd cycle fast through one aria and more slowly through the next. The change in intensity and focus always made the time go by faster and the process more enjoyable.

Luciano also helped me get my dissertation done. The deal I cut with myself was that I only had to sit at the computer and work through one side of a tape. As with the cycling, the hard part was getting started. Once I was working, I could keep going.

I sometimes psyche myself into an activity by focusing on how I'll feel if I don't do it. I ask myself if what I am avoiding is important to what I want to accomplish. A useful question I ask is, "What difference will this make in twenty years?" If I don't run today or write today, in twenty years it won't make any difference. But what if I get in the habit of skipping? So the reality is—what I do today makes a difference for my tomorrows. Indeed, the way I choose to live today is the foundation for tomorrow. If I want to live well tomorrow, I need to live well today.

Another question that I ask myself is "Will this make me proud of myself?" I know that I'll feel proud of myself if I do the writing, or make the phone calls, or eat my vegetables. I like being proud of myself much better than I like feeling let down by myself. If in each moment of my day, I behave in such a way that I'm proud of myself, I'll go to bed happy and content.

Taking positive action is an antidote to the negative self-statements most of us make to ourselves. Because of my childhood obesity, and because the culture that I live in has such a ridiculous standard for female thinness, my body image has been that I'm fat. The fact that I now have over twenty-five years of being physically active under my belt means that I'm very fit, healthy, and strong. The exercise has gradually changed my body image from "fat" to fit.

The physical strength and stamina that I've accrued generalizes to other parts of my life. Because I am physically strong, I know that I am mentally and emotionally strong as well. I can say to myself, "Because you have the strength to do x, you know you can find the strength to do y." When I was in labor with my second son, who weighed in at 9 pounds 10 3/4 ounces, I kept saying to myself, "Rita, this is just like one more hard lap on the track. You've done that, you can do this." It's wonderful to know that you have reserves of strength.

When I was 50, I discovered that I have a meningioma, a benign tumor on my brain. For three hellish weeks, I thought that I was going to be the guest of honor at brain surgery. It was useful to remind myself that I knew that I could get through it. I had trained myself to be disciplined and do hard things. It was also useful to know that my superior physical conditioning was going to make the whole process easier. Thankfully, I did not have to have the surgery and test it all out.

The fruit is, indeed, out there in the skinny branches. In order to pick it and eat it, we will be required to stretch, and reach, and grow. In the stretching, we will feel challenged and uncertain and unsafe. But when we have that plum in our hand, we can savor it, knowing that we've done the hard things and earned it. We can be proud of ourselves and pleased with the confidence that we've gained. And we can look up and see another fruit hanging higher in the tree and laugh delightedly as

Unlock Your Possibilities

we begin to make plans to "commit to it and go." Living in the skinny branches is living!

Action Steps

1. Change something about your daily routine: Take a different route to work, experiment with a different style of dress, take a class just because the subject interests you.

2. Choose something that seems difficult to you: Introducing yourself first to strangers at a meeting, or volunteering to head the next project at work, or if you've always volunteered to head the projects, don't volunteer. Then follow through and take action on your choice.

3. Write a poem, the theme of which is what thoughts, actions, and behaviors you can engage in which will improve the overall quality of your life. Remember, it does not matter if you've ever written a poem before or not. Just commit to it and go.

4. Without stopping, write a "Personal Scared-y Cat" list of the things that you fear. Write down as many as you can think of, without stopping. Brainstorm. Just let the fears flow out of you. Once you are conscious of the fears that act like strings around your leg, you are in position to take action to move through the fear. Once this task is complete, other fears may surface. Don't be afraid.

5. Choose one of the fears from the list above and create an affirmation which refutes it. For example, if you wrote, "I am afraid to be alone," an affirmation might be "I am content and happy by myself and know that I possess all the skills and knowledge that I need to manage my life successfully."

6. Choose one of the fears and create an action plan to overcome it. For example, "I am afraid to fly" might be a fear. The action plan would be a program that is called systematic desensitization. The process is one of creating a list of the steps you would need to make to fly in a plane. Those steps might include calling the airline to get ticket schedules and prices, going to the airport, parking your car, and taking one of the courses to help people overcome their fear of flying. The first step you list should be one that you can imagine doing without experiencing any tension or anxiety. If you don't currently know how to consciously relax, you will need to master that skill first. You arrange your list of necessary steps in sequence, then simultaneously imagine doing the step and being completely realized at the same time. When you can do the first step without any tension, you move to imagining the second step until you can imagine doing that in a completely relaxed state. Whenever you feel tension, shift your attention to the previous item and regain your relaxation. Once you have gone through the list and can imagine doing each and every step in a relaxed state start actually doing the steps, again stopping when you feel anxious and focusing on being relaxed. You will be able to desensitize yourself to the fear and not allow it to trap you in the status quo.

Points to Ponder
- Take action and master the fear. Do nothing and the fear masters you.
- Being fearful is a choice.
- Our thoughts can imprison us. Our thoughts can set us free.
- An heroic life is created one decision at a time.

Chapter 8

FIT AND FABULOUS! PUTTING MORE LIFE IN YOUR LIFESTYLE

A FEW WEEKS AGO, *a business friend, Peg, told me about the fifty mile ultra run that she was planning to do. The race route was fifty miles of woodland trails that crossed through my hometown at the twenty mile point. Peg lives over an hour's drive from the race site and the race was scheduled to begin at 7 A.M. My experience as a triathlete gave me an instant understanding that Peg was going to need to get up at about 3:30 A.M. in order to get to the race start, so I quite spontaneously asked if she wanted to stay with me the night before the race. She did and then causally inquired if I might want to pace her for part of the race. After twenty miles she told me race rules allowed her to have someone run along with her. It sounded like fun, so I said, "Sure."*

My plan was to pick her up in the center of town, accompany her through the woods to the road, run back to my car, drive to the next town, run with her for a while, then go back to my car and hopscotch to the next meeting point. I planned on running a total of six to eight miles with her, with most of them in the 40 to 50 mile part of her race, a time when she would be tired and get the greatest benefit from having me pace her.

At the appointed time, I waited for her to run out of the woods into town. She arrived, looking fresh and feeling good. She took the time to eat and drink and then we were off on a gloriously beautiful June day, running along a New England woodland path. Her race plan was to run the flats and downhills, then walk the uphills. The pace was easy and we ran, chatting and comparing notes with Mark, a younger man who was running his first ultra distance race. After three to four miles we emerged into the road; they crossed over and disappeared into the woods as I turned and ran back to my car. This was fun!

After grabbing a peanut butter sandwich and a gallon of water, I drove to North Andover, found the road crossing I was looking for, and waited for Peg and Mark to arrive. Within a short time, they showed up, grinning, and we headed up the hill back into the woods. It was such a beautiful day. The sun dappled across the forest floor. The trees were wearing their best shade of fresh green. Lady slippers bloomed at intervals along the trails edge. Birds happily reminded us that it was spring.

We ran for three to four miles, getting lost because the trail wasn't very well marked and had to back track. I began to wonder when I should turn back to get to my car and hopscotch again. I began to think that I was so far from my car that it made more sense to stop at one of the aid stations and ask someone with a car to drive me back. With that plan in mind, I continued running.

The aid stations that I came upon weren't manned with enough people to give me a hitch back; I was feeling great and enjoying myself enormously. I was weighing what I should do as I ran happily along. I was acutely aware that the most I had run at a time in the past year and a half was 6 miles. I was over that distance. Was it smart to keep going? Was I risking really straining muscles or causing myself serious injury? But, how was I going to get back to my car?

Somewhere in the woods of North Andover, my plan switched. I decided to run to the end of the race as long as I kept feeling good. I promised myself to carefully monitor my body. If I decided that if I was pushing myself too far, I would simply stop at one of the aid stations and ask for assistance. My plan in place, I mentally settled in for the long haul.

The afternoon passed in a flash. I was in the flow, with no sense of time, immersed in the rhythms and power of my body and the beauty of the surroundings. Peg and I talked at times, easy relaxed conversation. Several times we got lost. The trail markers continued to be hard to find. The race route went through some streets as well as through the woods. The junctions of roads and woods caused problems for many of us. The first couple of times it happened, our attitudes were accepting. That was just the way it was. We searched until we found the trail without being bothered by the confusion. As the miles wore on, the frustration of spending extra steps grew. It was no longer okay to be doing those diversions. Both of us agreed that it was psy-

chologically very helpful to be with the other. It would have been very difficult to manage without company.

I continued to monitor my body. I could feel some tension in my right hamstring which had been cranky over the spring, but the discomfort never moved to pain. I felt okay about continuing. I took the time to stretch at each of the aid stations and made sure that I was eating and drinking enough. We came to the final stretch of roadway, finished that, and moved into the woods, running along a trail that skirted the Merrimac River. Absolutely beautiful! The last half mile or so, I felt my body starting to "hit the wall" and I knew that I had reached the limits of my safe endurance. But I had only a half mile to go and I knew I would cross the finish line with Peg, having had a great, satisfying, and unexpected adventure.

I crossed the finish line and headed for the food. What enormous satisfaction! I was fifty-five years old and had just run somewhere between 28 and 30 miles—easily. I had done it on the basis of all the years that I have kept myself in good physical shape. All those years of dedicated exercise were deposits into my endurance account. I had demonstrated to myself that I could tap into the account in a major way and draw only on some of the interest. The account has not been touched. It is still there, growing and compounding everyday. It felt so good to tap into the strength and power of my physical body. How deeply, deeply satisfying to know that I had all that capacity, all that endurance and stamina. How absolutely delightful to know that although I qualify for a senior citizen's bank account, there's nothing old about me. I may be chronologically aging, but I'm not getting old!

Thanks, Peg, for inviting me into a very satisfying adventure!

You can't live a first class life in a third-rate body. With your body, there is nothing truer than *Use It or Lose It*. America has become the land of the free and the home of the soft. We delude ourselves that we can have it both ways—fitness and health with no investment. We don't really believe that we can have a fat bank account (well, maybe we do, given the popularity of gambling in this country) without saving regularly. Gambling your way to wealth has just about the same probability of success as sitting your way to health.

In the early seventies when I started running, virtually no one else was running. There were a few of those "weird" guys who ran marathons on the roads, but I never saw another woman. Sometimes, friends and acquaintances would ask, with unconcealed skepticism, "Do you think you're going to live longer because you do that?" My answer then was, "I don't know if I'm going to live longer but I do know that I'm going to live better." What I didn't understand from the vantage point of being in my early thirties was how much better "better" was going to get.

When I was in my early thirties, there wasn't much difference between my capacity and that of my peers. Now, at the age of fifty-five, there is a phenomenal difference. I know that when I am seventy-five and many of my age group are infirm, disabled, or dead, I'll still be riding my bike and climbing mountains. I now know that my exercising will not only add years to my life, but life to my years.

The health of this country is appalling in the light of the resources and knowledge that we have. For much of the nineties there has been great deal of media attention to the issue of "health care." What we are calling "health care" in this country is a misnomer. It's not health care! It's disease care! It's fixing what's broken, not prevention. It wouldn't make any sense to know that your car is leaking oil and not take it in and at least fill up the oil reservoir. No one in his or her right mind would deliberately let the oil level get so low that the motor seized up. Yet, that's what millions of us do with our bodies. We know that we don't have the physical stamina that we did when we were younger or we know that our cholesterol levels are too high or that the big paunch we've acquired is not good for our back muscles and is a sign that we could be in danger of a heart attack. Those are all signs that our oil levels are low. Yet, we keep right on driving ourselves, staying in denial until the day they cart us off to the emergency room—or to the morgue. Even then, the survivors don't really take the message to *heart*. Many of them start to exercise, or quit smoking, or try to lose weight, but lose the focus and revert to the old "killer" habits. What a shame!

I don't know about you but death and illness are experiences that I'd like to delay as long as possible. I've been ill before, not seriously and not for long, but having tried it, I can tell you quite honestly that I don't like it! I think it's a waste of time. I've not done death before (that I'm aware of!). Maybe it's not as bad as it seems. Maybe it's another part of a great unfolding adventure and it will be a fabulous experience. However, I can wait! My preference would be to wait for many, many years. If there's something I can do about delaying the inevitable, I will do it. That means that I will be out there running through the dawn for decades to come. That means I will maintain control of my tongue which absolutely loves the taste and feel of food. That means I will take the time to make sure that I get adequate rest. That means I will (mostly) eat the foods that are healthy for me, not the ones that just taste good and don't nourish me. That all means I am one of a small minority in the United States.

Let's look at some of the statistics. I weigh less than I did when I was in the fourth grade. My blood pressure runs about 100/60. My resting pulse is 45 and has been for years. My cholesterol level is in the 170s. My energy level is high. I am proud of my body in a country where most women hate theirs. People consistently think that I am 10 -15 years younger than I am. When I was 52, someone asked a friend, "How old is she anyhow, in her early thirties?" Now ask me if you think the results justify the effort?

Let's look at some more statistics. According to the July/August 1996 issue of *Health*, 69% of Americans say they are satisfied with their level of fitness; only 27% follow the surgeon general's recommendation for minimum physical fitness (that's exercising aerobically three times a week for twenty minutes). The Tufts University *Health & Nutrition Letter* (June 1997, Vol. 15, No. 4) states that one third of men and almost half of the women in this country say they rarely or never work up a sweat. We've created so many labor-saving devices, it seems that most of us are trying to live our lives as out-of-body experiences!

Obesity rates are soaring with one third of American adults being classified as medically obese. The obesity rate among children is higher that it has ever been, probably in the history of the human race. Dr. Walter Willet of the Harvard Medical School has termed our dietary habits the "worst in the history of the world." What an outrage! We have the most plentiful food supply of any civilization in the history of the world—and we feed ourselves junk! We're flunking nutrition, one of the core courses for a healthy life.

The Tufts University *Health & Nutrition Letter* (ibid.) published the results of the United States Department of Agriculture's findings on the eating habits of Americans. Fewer than half of us eat the recommended three servings of vegetables per day. And 40% of the vegetables we do eat are potatoes. Only one person in ten eats a dark green or yellow vegetable per day. Those are the vegetables that come loaded with the antioxidants that promote health and longevity. Three out of four Americans do not get the minimum of two servings of fruit per day. Not only are we not eating the foods that are healthy for us, we are overloading on those that are nutritionally a waste. Americans get 40% of their calories from sugar and fats. That means we're only getting nutritional value from the remaining 60% of our calories. It takes 1200 calories per day to get all the basic nutrients we need. Many women try to live on 1200 or fewer calories per day in order to keep their weight down (obviously, it's not working). Sixty percent of 1200 calories is 720 calories. That's not enough to maintain health.

Zig Ziglar, the motivational speaker, asks audiences if they had a race horse that was worth a million dollars, how would they take care of it? The answer is, of course, that everyone would make sure that the animal got the very best food available and the right amount of rest balanced by the right amount of exercise. Don't we all think our lives are worth a million dollars?

THE BENEFITS OF EXERCISE

Have you ever thought about the benefits of exercise? The following is a partial list of the physical **(P)** and emotional **(E)** benefits of regular exercise.

- **(P)** • lose fat
- **(P)** • lowered risk of stroke
- **(P)** • increased muscle tone and definition
- **(P)** • have more energy
- **(P)** • sleep better
- **(P)** • more youthful appearance
- **(P)** • feel stronger
- **(E)** • reduced stress
- **(E)** • have less anxiety
- **(P)** • have increased productivity
- **(P)** • improved digestion
- **(E)** • increased confidence
- **(P)** • reduced back pain
- **(P)** • increased endurance
- **(P)** • better posture
- **(P)** • improved athletic performance

- **(P)** • decreased chance of injury
- **(P)** • improved circulation
- **(P)** • better fitting clothes
- **(P)** • enhanced sex life (and **(E)**!)
- **(P)** • stronger heart muscle
- **(E)** • increased creativity
- **(P)** • improved circulation
- **(P)** • better skin
- **(P)** • possibly, headache relief
- **(P)** • lower blood pressure.
- **(P)** • decreased risk of heart disease
- **(P)** • decreased risk of diabetes
- **(P)** • quicker recovery from pregnancy or surgery
- **(P)** • reduced risk of osteoporosis
- **(P)** • increased bone density
- **(P)** • slowed joint degeneration
- **(P)** • better joint flexibility
- **(P)** • stronger immune system
- **(P)** • maintain or gain muscle mass
- **(P)** • lower heart rate
- **(P)** • increased range of motion
- **(E)** • improved memory
- **(P)** • possible reduced substance abuse
- **(P)** • increased metabolic rate
- **(P)** • reduced likelihood of some forms of cancer, including breast and colon
- **(P)** • enhanced use of oxygen
- **(P)** • improved reaction time
- **(P)** • reduced risk of gynecological problems
- **(P)** • reduced incidence of painful menstruation
- **(P)** • maintenance of independence for more years
- **(P)** • improved nervous system functioning
- **(P)** • improved longevity
- **(E)** • improved intelligence, in the elderly
- **(E)** • effective treatment of depression
- **(P)** • reduced risk of hospitalization at the end of life

| Unlock Your Possibilities |

QUESTION: If I had a drug that would do all these things for you, what would you pay me for it?
ANSWER: Anything that I asked! And I wouldn't have a marketing budget either.

There is ample evidence that you don't have to be hardcore and fanatic about exercise to gain benefits. The three thirty minute aerobic exercise sessions recommended for heart health do not even have to be done thirty minutes at a time. It seems that you can break the sessions up into ten minute blocks and still get the benefit. Studies have shown that the incidental exercise of housework and gardening provide benefit. It certainly is nice that they've discovered some benefit from housecleaning! Research evidence has found that five minutes of sit-ups, leg, and back exercises made a difference in abdominal strength, flexibility, and increased self-esteem in twelve weeks. That's only a total of seven hours in three months for a measurable increase in fitness. What a bargain. So much return for so little investment.

TYPES OF EXERCISE NEEDED FOR OPTIMAL HEALTH

People sometimes ask, "What muscles do I need to exercise?" My flip answer is, "Only the ones you want to keep." The truth of the matter is that after maturity when growth ceases, the body will start to deteriorate. The rate of deterioration in our twenties or thirties is usually slow enough so that we don't really notice a difference. When people are in their forties, the deterioration becomes more evident. Unless we provide our bodies with the nourishment and the movement that they need, the deterioration is inevitable. Providing the exercise and nourishment your body needs slows the deterioration remarkably. When I was thirty-eight, I came back from an early morning run. My cousin, Ruth, said to me, "That body doesn't look like it's thirty-eight years old!" Almost twenty years later, it still doesn't. Recently a eighteen-year old commented that my body looked like I was in my twenties.

There are three different types of exercise that your body needs for maximum health and vitality—aerobic, strengthening, and stretching. Aerobic exercise is the type that gets you, your breath, and your heart rate moving faster. Walking, cross-country skiing, swimming, cycling, running, dancing, and aerobics are all forms of aerobic exercise. As mentioned above, for heart health, all you need to do is 30 minutes, three times per week. Less than one percent of your week is all it takes to keep your heart healthy. If your goal is to lose body weight, it makes sense to increase the time you spend exercising up to one hour per day. The longer periods of exercise give your body more time in its most efficient fat-burning mode. You will gain an additional benefit from the higher rate of metabolic burn that lasts for several hours after you've finished exercising. One of the most effective weight loss research projects that I encountered while doing my dissertation research was done in the very early 1970s. A researcher named Gwinup started a group of women on a walking program, building them up until they were walking for one hour per day. They were not placed on a diet. At the end of the year, those who had stayed with the program (two thirds dropped out) had lost an average of thirty-five pounds. Those are still outstanding results for obesity research. Exercise is a powerful treatment for obesity and overweight.

The second type of exercise needed for maximum health is strengthening or weight training. Strengthening should be done no more than every other day. The stress that you place on the muscles breaks down the fibers microscopically. Over the next day, the muscle rebuilds the fibers, making them stronger. Many women are reluctant to use weights. Part of the reason is that it moves them out of their comfort zones to even consider being seen in a health club or gym with all those sleek looking people who know what they are doing. It isn't necessary to do that. Your body is a great set of weights. You can learn lots of weight lifting exercises using only your body. Other potential weights are found in your kitchen. Soft drink bottles and vegetable cans can be used when you first start. I recommend that you get someone who knows how to lift to show you how to lift. You'll get much more benefit from the work if you are doing it correctly and you are less likely to hurt yourself.

One of the major benefits of weight lifting is that you will put additional muscle on your body. Muscle is metabolically active tissue. That means it burns calories—up to fifty calories per day per pound of added muscle. By increasing your muscle mass, you can actually increase the number of calories your body requires to maintain itself each day. Most women can put up to ten pounds of muscle on their bodies. We have great potential for adding muscle on our upper bodies, which tend to be relatively under-developed and weak on women. The great news in that is that adding muscle to your arms and shoulders tends to balance out your figure so that your hips don't appear as wide. I've rarely met a woman who didn't think it would be a great idea to make her hips look smaller.

A concern that women sometimes express about weight lifting is that they'll look like Arnold Schwarzenegger. Not so! Women don't have enough testosterone to build the kind of bulky muscles that men do. In addition to the metabolic advantage that additional muscle gives, weight training has been shown to reduce the risk of osteoporosis in post-menopausal women. Instead of losing bone after menopause, weight training is a way of actual building it.

FLEXIBILITY

This is my favorite type of exercise. If you are over the age of thirty and haven't been stretching regularly, you probably have noticed that you aren't as flexible as you were when you were younger. When you try to reach your toes, somehow the floor is farther away than it used to be. Stretching is the cure for that. Stretching can and should be done every day. It needn't take more than ten or fifteen minutes (I can hear you saying, "Is she crazy? I have too much to do to put this much time into exercising"). My very favorite form of stretching is yoga which I wholeheartedly recommend to anyone and everyone. It is very relaxing—an antidote to the stressed-out world in which we live. It is also a strengthening activity because you are using muscles all over your body to hold yourself in the positions. Because our mind/bodies do not snap apart, because they are totally integrated, doing yoga is also a way to make your mind more flexible.

I vividly remember the first yoga class I attended. Nancy, the instructor, started by teaching us sun salutation and then moved into other postures. About thirty minutes into the class, I had a sudden realization, "I feel great!" What I noticed was a relaxed alertness. It's a great feeling that I get every time I do yoga. If you choose not to try yoga, it is still important to make the effort to stretch all your muscles frequently.

You don't have to set aside a separate time for the stretching. I put my foot up on the bathroom window sill and stretch while I am drying my legs after my morning shower. I stretch my arms and shoulders while sitting at traffic lights. While sitting at the computer, I take neck breaks and stretch my neck by rolling my head from side to side across my chest. Another computer stretch I do is to push back my chair and simply fold my body forward across the tops of my thighs and let my hands dangle on the floor. Another stretch is to push back in my chair and hold onto the edge of my desk while pushing my hips back in my chair. This stretches the whole length of my back. The stretches you can do are limited only by your imagination. One of the nicest things about stretching is that you don't have to wait for weeks to see the benefit. You'll see it immediately.

CHANGING EATING HABITS

I went on my first diet when I was thirteen. I had suffered from the obesity of my childhood and at thirteen had become very self conscious. My first diet consisted of refusing desserts and not snacking. That was one of my most successful diets. I lost weight and was faithful to it for three months. From then until I was thirty and discovered running, dieting was a way of life for me. I was always hungry, deprived, and unsuccessful. When I was in my mid-twenties, I dieted successfully and actually got down to 125, which was my "magic number," the one I'd dreamed of making for years. I stayed there for fifteen minutes! Learning to run was the ticket to freedom from dieting domination. I will never go on a diet again.

Many people seem to be on what I call the dieter's pendulum. Does this sound familiar? You get up one morning and get on the scale, look at the number in horror and decide you can't stand it anymore. You're going to lose weight! That decision triggers a regimen that would make the ancient Greeks tremble. The diet that ensues is so difficult to stick to that, even though some of the weight comes off, the program is unbearable for the long run. Something happens and the diet is violated—then it's "if it doesn't move I'll eat it" time. You then move into the non-diet phase where there are no rules. The exercise program ceases. Your weight quickly goes up, and your self-esteem just as quickly goes down. You stay on the non-dieting end of the pendulum until you can't stand that anymore and switch back to diet mode. And the endless cycle begins again.

There is an expression that I'm fond of—do what you always did, get what you always got. If what you've been doing to manage your weight hasn't been working, doesn't it make sense that it's not going to work this time either? The weight loss prescription for the past decade has been a low-fat, high-carbohydrate regimen. Our supermarkets shelves are laden with no-fat, low-fat, reduced-fat items. We've become obsessive about fat grams. And we've gotten fatter and fatter.

Until recently, the low-fat, high-carbohydrate plan was the one I followed. A year and a half ago, for reasons unrelated to weight control, I started using the Zone food plan developed by Barry Sears. I followed it very closely for three months. In that time I lost 10 pounds—easily. I was less troubled by food cravings that at any time since I was seven years old. Just before starting the Zone I had had my thyroid checked because I was falling asleep in the evening. My hormone levels were fine, but after I started living in the Zone, I noticed that I no longer fell asleep at night. In fact, I noticed I had more energy than ever. I also noticed that it was very easy to gain strength with my weight lifting. I constantly needed to keep increasing the amount of weight I was using. For me, eating in the Zone is the most comfortable way to eat that I have ever found in my life.

My experience with the Zone makes me reflect on the earliest dieting information I remember; bread, potatoes, and rice were "fattening." Overeater's Anonymous for years recommended staying away from "white" foods. Optifast was the most efficient way to lose weight (people didn't do very well with maintenance, probably because a low-fat, high-carbohydrate diet was recommended). That was a no-carbohydrate diet. It would be interesting to see how people would do with an Optifast/Zone regimen. These factors provide some interesting support for the utility of a lower carbohydrate, higher protein diet for weight loss—and weight-loss maintenance.

The reception of the medical community to the Zone diet has been lukewarm to hostile. It has received a lot of bad press. One of the misimpressions that has been promoted is that Zone eating is a license to eat lots of high-fat, high-cholesterol meals. That is not an accurate picture of the Zone. To eat healthfully on the Zone requires self-discipline and carefully choosing the foods you eat.

The major point of this: If the eating plan you've been following has not been working for you, perhaps it's time to open up your thinking and try a different strategy. One of the most counter-productive features of our humanity is our reluctance to examine our premises and experiment with new ways of thinking and acting. If you continue to do the same old thing, you'll undoubtedly get the same old result.

SABOTEURS

When you move into a healthier lifestyle, taking charge of your eating and exercise habits, you are likely to encounter saboteurs. In fact, when you make any decision to improve your life and increase your level of achievement and happiness, the saboteurs will more than likely show up. I define a saboteur as anyone who feels opposed to, or ambivalent about, your changing. Saboteurs can be family, friends, co-workers, even yourself. People's reactions, including your own, about your success are likely to be mixed. The reactions are not intended to be hostile. Consciously, saboteurs would probably even say they are on your side and want you to succeed. They want you to have what you want for yourself. But, and it's a big "but," subconsciously, the saboteur is uneasy about the change that you are making. What are the implications for them? If you are successful with this change, what will the next one be? And if you keep changing, maybe you won't like them anymore and will go away and leave them alone. The basic, underlying fear of the saboteur is that good results in your life may create bad results for them. Inadvertently, when we change, we move the people around us out of their comfort zones into the skinny branches. People don't usually like to get taken out into the skinny branches by someone else's decisions or actions.

The best way to avoid getting into a struggle with the saboteurs is to communicate, communicate, communicate with them. Becoming conscious and communicating to them your understanding of their fears and concerns will get the concerns up on the table where they can be addressed. You can be very clear about what the implications are of the changes you are making—for them. When you, and they, are clear about where you're at, then you can problem-solve together on how to make the situation work for both or all of you. This process works whether it is the people external to you or the ones that live in your head.

It is possible that no matter how clear and reasonable you are about your decisions, other people in your life may be unwilling or unable to tolerate your changes. That is their responsibility, not yours. At that point, you will need to decide how much of **your life** you are willing to give away. You may decide to not change, but if you do, do it consciously with full awareness of the implications of what you are doing. If you decide that you are not going to exercise, make the decision in full light of the consequences, both long term as well as short term.

The decision to be healthier, to eat well and to exercise, is not a decision that you make once. It is a decision that you make over and over again. You make it each time you decide to put your shoes on and go for a walk. You make it each time you refuse that fat-laden chocolate dessert. You make it each time you insist that you are going to go to aerobics class even though the boss really wants you to stay a bit later at work.

The decision to eat right and exercise regularly is an investment that you make in yourself. It is a commitment to valuing your life. The word "investment" comes from the Latin *investire*, to commit for a long period with the thought of a future benefit. Making the investment of time and energy for your good health is one of the wisest investments that you'll ever make. Recently I took the shuttle from Boston to New York. During the flight I fell into a conversation with my seatmate. At one point, she asked how old I was, "About forty?" Well, yes, I'm about forty! The payoff is not just that I look so much younger than I am; the real payoff is that physiologically I *am* so much younger than I am.

Action Steps

1. If you are over the age of 35, consult you physician before engaging in an exercise program. It is also useful to consult with a dietitian for personal guidance in dietary changes.

2. Increase your physical activity by 5 minutes per day for one week. Even if you are doing nothing more strenuous than channel surfing now, 5 minutes a day is possible. Then add 5 minutes per week until you are moving for the 30 minutes three times per week.

3. You'll probably resist this suggestion, but it is one of the best techniques for increasing awareness about what you are eating. Choose three days this week (one of them a weekend day) and write down everything you eat. Don't change your eating habits, just record your food consumption. Then analyze it for fat, calorie, and nutrient content. Knowing what you are really eating is very valuable data for knowing what changes will lead to greater health for you.

4. Write a list of all the reasons why you want to lose weight or increase your level of fitness. Post it where you can read it frequently. It will help you stay focused on your goals.
5. Join a health club or weight loss program. Enlist the aid of an exercise buddy. Having an external source of support and encouragement is very useful when you are having difficulty finding your own motivation.
6. Spend five minutes per day stretching your body. Just move in any way that feels good.
7. Write reminders of your goals on Post-Its. Tack them on your bathroom mirror or on your refrigerator or on the dashboard of your car.
8. Set up a reward system for yourself. Give yourself X number of points for meeting your daily exercise goal or following your eating plan. Each point is converted into a dollar amount. When you've achieved a predetermined amount of money, buy yourself a treat (not chocolate!).

Points to Ponder

- Knowledge is power. Knowledge without action is useless.
- Your body—if you don't have one you are not only out of the running—you are out of this life.
- Don't ask if you have to exercise for the rest of your life. Hope that you can.
- Maintaining a difficult yoga posture encourages me to know that I can maintain a difficult mental or emotional posture.
- No one dies unexpectedly.
- You can either waste extra food or waist extra food
- Exercise reduces stress, increases immune functioning, prevents diabetes, heart disease, osteoporosis, aids in weight control, promotes sleep, and prevents constipation as well as relieves depression and increases self-esteem. If I had a drug that would do that, what would you pay me?
- Your body is only as strong as its weakest cell.

Chapter 9

ADDRESS YOUR STRESS: GETTING COOL, CALM AND CONNECTED

I COULD FEEL the warm spring sun on my back as I climbed White Horse Ledge. New to rock-climbing, I really enjoyed the adventure. I loved being outdoors. I loved the intensity of the physical challenge, the mental game of figuring out the moves I needed to make, the process of discovering whether I had the physical strength and technique to successfully execute them. I loved being in a flow state, with no awareness of time, no thoughts about what was going on in my "real life," just fully living in the moment.

As I climbed, I thought back to my first climbing experience a few months before. The very first route I climbed had started in a gully, moved up past some trees and then out onto the open rock face. I had climbed easily out from behind the trees. Once out onto the face, I'd decided to look out behind me so that I could take advantage of the view. I'd turned, looked over my right shoulder, and felt a wash of fear roar through my body. Quickly, I turned to reface the cliff and decided I would sightsee later, after I had reached the top of the cliff. I thought about how quickly I had gotten comfortable on the cliffs.

I was climbing easily that morning, enjoying my strength and my competence. We came to a place where there was a big block (a ledge that was almost two feet wide), and I had to step across to another block, equally wide. The handholds that were available were big, in the vernacular of climbers, "buckets." The physical challenge was no more difficult than stepping from one rock to another as I crossed a stream. The mental challenge was overwhelming. There was nothing below the two blocks but 200 feet of air.

UNLOCK YOUR POSSIBILITIES

I stood on the block looking across the abyss, wondering how I was going to come up with the courage to cross. I was in no real danger. I was on belay; Joe had the rope snugly held. I checked the figure-eight knot that secured my rope to my harness. Even if I fell, I was going nowhere. I would hang safely from the equipment. The risk was all in how I perceived the situation. I was in a classic approach-avoidance situation and vacillated about the decision to move across the space. I knew that I didn't want to spend the rest of my life on the face of White Horse Ledge, so not making the move really wasn't an option. Still, I hesitated—and hesitated.

The climber's expression, "Commit to it and go," kept going through my mind. I'd get to the verge of making the step and then back off. I don't know how many times I decided to go and then backed away. My years of teaching stress management classes began to assert themselves. I coached myself to "Breathe deeply. Relax, relax, relax." As I said the words, I could feel my body letting go of some of the fear. I could feel myself getting more focused and regaining control of my runaway fears. I screwed up my courage and stepped easily across.

A few years later, I sat in the office of a neurosurgeon and listened to him tell me that I had a benign tumor on the surface of my brain and that it needed to come out immediately. It was in danger of encroaching on major blood vessels and that unremoved, the tumor was a threat to my life. Being a savvy medical consumer, I told him that I would be seeking a second opinion. Before I left the office, we scheduled a tentative date for the surgery—five days after I was to receive my doctorate.

I drove to my job at the Optifast clinic, reeling with the thought of brain surgery. As a nurse, I knew what goes on in neurosurgery. I remembered the sound that bone saws make cutting through skulls. I really found the whole idea most distasteful—and extremely frightening. I had no desire to be the guest of honor at brain surgery.

I arrived at work to find that my office had been moved. Indeed the whole clinic had been moved—and no one had informed us! I was scheduled to see two new patients that afternoon and the only thing left in my office was the phone, sitting on the window sill. It seems my boss had gone on vacation without telling us that they were going to move our offices to another part of the building. I canceled my afternoon appointments, told my boss's boss that I expected full pay for the day, and went home.

That evening I went back to the hospital and taught a community educa-

tion program—on stress management! The program I gave that night was very well received. No one ever knew that the person who most needed stress management in that class was the instructor. Just as I had on White Horse Ledge, I kept myself fully present and in the moment.

After three hellish weeks I learned that I did not need the surgery. I still have my meningioma and anticipate taking it with me to the next life. The ability to manage my stress was an invaluable aid in getting through that awful experience. I don't know if I'll ever again be as challenged by a stressful event in my life. I do know that the skills I have in managing myself in challenging circumstances are an invaluable resource for my life. Knowing that I am able to manage my emotional reactions to any situation or crisis keeps me anchored in myself and much freer to enjoy the experiences of my life.

Stress is as pervasive in the United States as chlorine in our drinking water. It is simply a part of the landscape that most of us accept as a given. Some of us even get into a competition for who can be the most stressed out, secretly taking pride in how much we can handle. We act as if it were normal to live in such a way that we are constantly destroying our bodies with the bath of biochemicals that stress releases. Some eighty percent of the diseases that hospitalize us have a stress connection. In the work setting, according to the Wellness Councils of America's report, *Healthy, Wealthy and Wise: Fundamentals of Workplace Health Promotion*, managers cited reduced productivity as the most serious consequence of stress. The estimate is that the average number of lost days from work due to stress, anxiety, and depression is 16 days per year. Another study found that seven in ten American workers said that stress was causing frequent health problems. Stress exacts an enormous toll on the energy, productivity, and happiness resources of this country every day. The amazing thing about this is that there is no such thing as stress in the environment. It doesn't exist "out there." It only exists in our reactions to and perceptions of what happens "out there" in the environment.

No event, problem, or situation in the Universe causes me stress. It is my interpretation of the events taking place that results in the stress reaction, the physiological changes in my body. Nothing in the world will cause me stress if I do not interpret it as threatening or dangerous.

Unlock Your Possibilities

Snakes almost universally elicit a fear response in humans. Not many of us want to hold and cuddle snakes, no matter how small and harmless. None of us was born fearing snakes. We learned to perceive them as dangerous. Indeed some of them are and a prudent human would make it a point to stay away from them. Shrieking in terror and running away from a garter snake, an animal that represents no threat to us whatsoever, is an unnecessary expenditure of the stress response.

Virtually none of us shrieks in terror and runs away from an automobile. Yet, automobiles are much more dangerous in the objective sense than snakes. Automobiles cause far more damage to life and limb than do snakes. Neither automobiles nor snakes are inherently stressful. It is our assessment of them that makes it so.

I sometimes wonder if the levels of stress that humans experience now are actually higher than that experienced by our predecessors of a hundred years ago. We certainly act as if that were so. Our forebears didn't keep the hectic, time-driven schedules that we do. But they experienced much more early death, and they worked long hard days, seven days per week. Many of them never took a vacation or traveled out of the town where they were born. They had no where near the level of comfort and affluence that we have in our lives. Yet, I suspect if I could time-travel back and engage them in a conversation about how they cope with stress, they would react to the concept of stress as if it were bizarre. I'd have to explain the concept to them.

So, why are we experiencing such high levels of stress? **Life has never been better for any civilization on the face of the earth than it is for Americans right now.** One of the reasons that we get so stressed is that we expect more than did previous generations. They expected that life would be hard and that they would always have problems and challenges to face. Somehow, we now seem to feel that life should be easy. We allow ourselves to feel stressed by the challenges that we face.

Another reason why we feel so stressed is that we walk around telling each other and ourselves how stressed we are. We talk all the time about how there isn't enough time or there isn't enough love or there isn't enough money. The problem with all these statements about being stressed is that we hear ourselves say them and believe what we say. They become self-fulfilling prophecies. Whatever you tell your subconscious mind, your subconscious believes. It is very important to watch what you say. Telling yourself that you are feeling calm, in control, and very relaxed will help make it so. Make it a habit to catch yourself when you are making one of those "not enough"statements and tell yourself instead that there is plenty. "I've got plenty of time, I've got plenty of love, I've got plenty of money." Even if those statements are not objectively true, you will feel more relaxed. Your stress will be reduced. The energy that you free up by being less stressed can then be applied to making those "plenty" statements come true.

Another factor that increases the stress level that we experience is the fast pace of life that we live. Most of us race through our days, frantically driven by the knowledge that we've got much more to do than time to do it in. We set impossibly high goals for ourselves, then get stressed out when we don't reach them. We work in jobs where the expectations and standards for productivity are extraordinarily high and frantically try to meet standards that can't be met. We then fear that we'll be fired if we don't meet those standards (this is not to deny the reality of how many people get downsized every year). The fear fuels the stress, the stress reduces productivity, which fuels the fear, etc. We get caught on a merry-go-round of stress and fear, all the while keeping the levels of stress hormones so high in our bodies that we are self-destructing, literally destroying body tissues. We vainly hope for the "someday" when things will ease up and life will get easier. We long for the day when we'll have time to do the things we want to do, rather than filling up our days with things we "have to do." Too many of us are so stressed about the things that we need to do today that we don't enjoy today. We look forward to retirement when we can take the time to do the things that we really enjoy. There are no guarantees that we'll live long enough to get to retirement—especially now when we are entering an era when retirement will be starting a new career. People in the future will be working later in life than sixty-five. If job stress is a many factor in your life, you need to either change your job or change your life.

When I say this to groups when I am speaking, the response usually is "I can't change my job," or "I don't have any choice, I have to go to work." My answer is that none of us "has" to go to work. We all *choose* to go to work. We may not like the consequences if we don't go, but to get up in the morning and go is always a choice.

Another reason that people feel so stressed today is that we are con-

Unlock Your Possibilities

stantly comparing ourselves to others—and seeing ourselves as coming up short. We act as if life was a game with someone keeping score. The awful t-shirt of the 80s that said "He who dies with the most toys wins" speaks to that idea. The truth is that there will always be someone younger, richer, better looking, taller, more intelligent, more successful. Measuring ourselves against others is a major waste of energy and a major source of stress.

"Success"—whatever that is—is a goal for which Americans strive. It is a rare person who doesn't want to be a success. We all want our children to be successful. There's nothing wrong with being successful. It's a great thing to want and have. The problem we have is that we keep moving our definition of success outward, so that we never allow ourselves to be successful. Then we come down on ourselves because we aren't successful enough. That makes no sense at all! If I have a standard of success that I can never reach, am I not setting myself up for lots of stress and tension?

There is an easy solution to this; just declare yourself as a "Success" no matter what you have or haven't achieved. Make your definition of success include only those things you've already done. It's your life. You get to set the standards and evaluate how you've met them. This approach is far less stressful than living your life with the unspoken belief that you don't measure up, you aren't "enough."

Most of us seem to have the idea that other people never have self-doubts. The idea is that there are people who "have it all together." I don't think so. I often ask audience members at my speeches to stand up if they never have self doubts. So far, no one ever has. The truth is we are all uncertain. If we were certain, we wouldn't be human, we'd be God. We increase our stress by needing to act as if we never encounter self-doubt. Only when we allow ourselves to be truthful and share our doubts and uncertainties with each other, can we can be genuine and real in our relationships. We can give up the stress engendered by needing to play a role.

Just as we can declare ourselves successful and relieve the stress of not having "made it," we can declare ourselves "good enough" and end the anxiety. You are of value just because you are. You do not have to justify your existence. This presupposes that you conduct yourself with honor. If you are a liar and a cheat and your value system says that it is not honorable to lie and cheat, you will know that you lack integrity. You can't compromise your integrity and still feel good about yourself. **You never lose when you maintain your integrity. You never win when you don't.**

PHYSIOLOGICAL RESPONSES TO STRESS

Imagine that you are in your bathroom late at night. No one else is home. You suddenly hear the sound of a window being broken and then intruders entering your home. As you hear the noise, you will automatically assume the "position of maximum readiness." This position is the same as the outfielders assume when the league leading batter stands up to the plate. Experiment with the position and observe the sensations that the position creates in your body. You should notice that the muscles in your arms and legs automatically tighten. When you first hear the breaking glass, you will stand still, your eyes will dilate. Your hearing will become more acute. Breathing becomes rapid and shallow. Your blood pressure and heart rate elevate. You may break out in a cold sweat. Digestive processes shut down, and you may experience the desire to use the bathroom. Your blood will clot more quickly, and you may have trouble thinking. You are now physiologically "dressed for stress." Within seconds every cell in your body has been affected and you are ready for "fight or flight."

This physiological response to danger is absolutely miraculous in its ability to prepare us to engage in massive physical action. It's the power that enables mothers to lift cars off small children or passers-by to rescue the occupants of a burning car. When you engage in physical action, the biochemical reactions move through their complete cycle. Fight or flight is a system designed for emergency use only. When the power is quickly charged and discharged, your body reverts to its normal physiological state easily and without harm.

What creates the stress "diseases" and causes bodily harm is continually triggering the response without the physical action. Making hand signals at the person who cuts you off at the traffic light *does not* constitute physical action! What happens is that your body is "all stressed up" with no place to go. Chronic stress causes the release of the hormone cortisol, which breaks down body tissue. Cortisol is a sign of a body being pushed too hard and not being given adequate recovery.

Most of the "dangers" that we perceive in our environments do not require a physical response. Being late for a flight or caught in traffic when we have a very important meeting does not require a physical response. On-the-job tensions with deadlines and cranky bosses do not require physical responses. Washing machines that break down and automated "customer service" menus that lead you through eighteen "press ones" before you learn that there is no way you can access a live human being do not call for physical responses. Humans today confront physical dangers only rarely. We live under a constant influx of psychological dangers which trigger our stress response dozens of times per day. The alarm that doesn't ring on time, the kids forgetting where they left their homework, the traffic jam on the way to work, the harried clerk at the drycleaners who rudely tells us that our cleaning won't be ready until tomorrow when we want to wear the garment tonight, the boss who piles on yet another big project...etc., etc., etc. With each one of those stimuli, the alarm goes off and our stress reaction is off and running.

RELIEF IS JUST A DEEP BREATH AWAY

You can exit from the road to di-stress using either your body or your mind. One of the quickest ways to cut through your stress response is to deliberately take slow, deep breaths. One of the reasons smokers get a relaxation response from their nicotine-laden (nicotine is a stimulant, not a relaxant) cigarettes is that when they inhale they take a long, slow, deep breath. The pace at which we live makes it a good practice to take deep breaths at least once every hour—and if you stretch at the same time, so much the better. Stress cause muscle fibers to shorten and tighten. Some of us keep them so tight and tense that we get muscle spasms and tension headaches. Stretching releases the tension. Relaxed muscles signal to the brain that all is well; it can turn off the alarm.

Here again, we need to monitor what we think, the messages we send to our bodies. When we think, "Oh, this is so awful! I'm so upset," your cells hear you. They will respond. A very valuable skill is to learn "don't sweat the small stuff,"—and to recognize that it's all small stuff. As a young woman, I devised a stress reducing question that has been invaluable to me over the years. The question that I ask myself when I am upset about something is, "In twenty years will this make a difference?" If the answer is, "No," then I choose to stop being upset. If the answer is, "Yes, this will be important in twenty years," then I know that I need to do some problem-solving or decision-making about the situation. Worrying about it won't help. In fact, it will make the situation worse.

One very powerful way to reduce stress is to recognize that you can choose how you react to a situation. There is a human tendency to "catastrophize" as Albert Ellis phrases it. Catastrophizing is magnifying the bad parts of a situation. Teenagers are quite expert at catastrophizing. Comments like, "I'll *never* be able to pass this math course," or "I'll just die if I don't get a date for Saturday night!" are catastrophizing. Adults catastrophize as well. We just tend to be more subtle about it—usually.

Catastrophizing is detrimental on two counts. First it sets up a self-fulfilling prophecy situation. I tell myself things are going to be awful and then I look for evidence to support that contention. If I'm looking, I'll find it. The second way catastrophizing is detrimental is that it consumes energy and focus that could be used in coming up with a good resolution for what is causing the stress. When you are upset about something, instead of catastrophizing ask yourself, "What could be good, useful, or beneficial about this situation?" When you are looking for something good in any situation, you will probably find it.

Several years ago, I taught myself a lesson in how I can control my reactions and create a positive outcome to a negative situation. I owned a wonderful pair of purple shoes that I loved. I had looked for them for three months before I found them. After much wearing, they needed repair and I took them to the cobbler, who was an elderly man (did you ever notice that cobblers always seem to be older?). The next week, I returned to the shop to pick up my shoes. The cobbler's wife who was manning the front desk took my ticket and disappeared behind the curtains to retrieve my shoes. I was running the typical Saturday-morning-working-mother routine, and I had at least seven things more on my schedule than I could possibly get done. Several minutes passed and the woman did not return with my shoes. I began getting frustrated and angry. I didn't have time for this delay! More time passed and I could feel the physiological changes that accompany anger getting stronger and stronger in my body. Where was she? And why wasn't she bringing my shoes to me? She came out and told me that she couldn't find my shoes. I wanted to bite her head off and vent my frustration. Instead, I decided

UNLOCK YOUR POSSIBILITIES

to be understanding and said, "Well, I've made a mistake before, too." She looked relieved and went back behind the curtains to continue the search. Several minutes later, she emerged to tell me that she thought my shoes had gone out the door with the gentleman who left as I came into the shop. She called his home, but he wasn't there. My anger was no longer there either. I had made a choice to be pleasant and friendly. After all who hasn't made a mistake? The woman said that she would call the man, get the shoes returned and mail them to me. That's what happened. The worst thing about this experience? I went another week without the shoes, and I stood in the shop for a few extra minutes.

As I left the shop that day the cobbler's wife thought I was wonderful because I was so understanding and nice about the mistake. She smiled and thanked me profusely. I left the shop that day feeling wonderful also. I had made a choice—a choice that left us both smiling and feeling good. I had avoided causing her unnecessary pain—always a good choice. Whatever the situation is that is causing you stress, you have a choice about how you react.

STRESS RELIEVER MENU

The following is a list of activities that are good for relieving stress:
- Deep breathing
- Progressive muscle relaxation
- Meditation
- Yoga*
- Exercise*
- Massage
- Sex
- Talking with a friend
- Watching the ocean
- Rocking in a chair
- Getting a back rub
- Singing
- Writing a loving note
- Re-reading old letters
- Taking a hot shower or bath
- Saunas
- Steam rooms

- Hot tubs
- Vacations
- Daydreams about vacations
- Stretching
- Reading
- Patting a dog or cat
- Watching a funny movie
- Holding a baby
- Driving
- Hypnosis
- Getting a manicure
- Shopping
- Taking a nap
- Having a facial
- Listening to, or playing, music
- Visualization exercises
- Dancing
- Making a decision
- Problem-solving
- Eating a favorite childhood food (go easy on this one!)
- Writing a list of all the good things in your life
- Smelling the pleasant smells of your childhood
- Spending some time alone in a beautiful place
- Massaging your feet
- Getting your hair done

*These are the best ways to relieve stress as far as I am concerned.

Problem-solving and decision-making bear some discussion. We make ourselves crazy trying to make up our minds about something. Being in a state of indecision is, in and of itself, stress-provoking (particularly if we don't give ourselves permission not to know)—like me wavering back and forth about whether I was going to move across from one of those rock blocks to the other or not. Sometimes I don't have all the information that I would like before I make a decision. Usually once I have made the decision and started to move on it, I find the additional information that I need—or I create it. Very few decisions in life are irrevocable. Most can be amended and reworked later if need be.

The decisions that are irrevocable you need to make with the utmost care and with all possible information. The other ones you can feel more free to experiment with. Even if you make a decision that turns out "wrong," you've learned what doesn't work. That's a positive.

The decisions that are irrevocable need to be made with the utmost of care and with all the possible information you can get. All others can be made much more freely, with an attitude of experimentation; if it doesn't work this way, then I'll try that way and if that still doesn't work, I'll keep tweaking it till it does. If you adopt the attitude that there's not a "right way" or a "wrong way" for you to live your life, and that no one's keeping score (least of all you), you will be much more relaxed as you follow your life's path.

In any stressful situation, there are the **FACTS**, the reality. The mortgage payment is…My daughter's grade in algebra is… Those are facts. We need to distinguish fact from our judgments. We tend to take data and then jump to conclusions. If you finish the mortgage statement with "and I'll never have the money for it," you are expressing an opinion. If you say "…and she'll never get into college," you're offering a judgment. Very often it's the judgment that we make that cause us stress, not the actual data. Not only does the judgment cause us increased stress, that type of statement is programming your sub-conscious to create the very result you fear. Result: Your stress increases and you get the result you don't want, which causes more stress, and round and round you go.

One of the ways that we increase our stress is to start with a bit of data and then embellish it. When we don't have the data we fill in the blanks by making things up. If you're in the workforce, you are well acquainted with this phenomenon. Very rarely does management tell the truth—the whole truth—about the situation. The workforce rarely feels they are being fully informed. What happens? When an organization is undergoing change, the rumor mill cranks up to high speed. The rumors do not allay fear and anxiety. Quite the opposite, they fan the flames of fear and the stress level goes up.

Stress in an organization or any group tends to spread like fire though a dry forest. Stress is catching. As we interact with people who are stressed, we catch the stress just as we "catch" a cold. We, in turn communicate our stress to the people we interact with. Result: The organization's stress increases which increases the incidence of irritability and fear, which increases the stress.... When we are coping with a stressful situation, it is a good idea to step back and ask: "What's fact here? What's fiction?" It makes no sense to react to the fiction; it's a waste of time, energy, and good body biochemicals. Instead of reacting, take the time and discover the data.

The second part of the stress chain is our **EMOTION**. When we hear that there have been break-ins in our neighborhood or that we didn't get the promotion we wanted or that we've got to work late for the fourth night in a row, we react emotionally. The reaction is usually a global reaction, a generalized negative feeling state. The negative emotion is itself perceived as a further stressor. Result: We get upset by the news, then we get further upset by our emotional reaction to the news, and round and round we go....

I have found it very useful to ask myself in a situation of stress, "Why am I reacting like this? Is this the way I want to react/feel? Is there a more positive way that I can choose to react?" My goal as I deal with the emotion is to shift out of a negative state into a positive state. There are three reasons for this. I don't like feeling negative emotion because negative emotion creates friction and wear and tear on both my body and my relationships, and negative thoughts and feelings can only create negative results and more stress.

Give yourself permission to feel whatever it is that you feel. Freely explore your emotions. An excellent strategy is to write about what you are experiencing. Studies have shown that writing about a stressor actually changes physiology and boosts immune functioning. What are you feeling? Are you angry? At yourself? At others? Raging? Sad? Guilty? Overwhelmed? All of the above? It is useful to know what your emotions are. It is equally useful to know that you don't want to make decisions based on your emotions.

We tend to make bad judgments when emotion is the driver. We meet someone and fall madly in love or in lust and make a lifelong commitment to that person without carefully exploring what the person's values are. We take a job because we are afraid of being out of work and end up miserably unhappy in the job. We say things in anger, lashing out at the people we most love. Giving yourself permission to feel your emotions does not mean that you will lose control. Quite the opposite.

Having felt and owned your emotions will increase the likelihood that when you express them you will be calm and in control. That increases the odds that the expression of emotion will bring intimacy, closeness, and understanding rather than dissension and distress.

The next step in addressing your stress is **ASSESSMENT**. In the assessment phase, you can ask questions like; "What are the possible implications of this data (don't forget to include possible positive results)? What can I learn from this situation? Are there opportunities this situation is pointing out? What are the options I have for dealing with it? What are my resources for remaining calm, relaxed, and focused? What steps do I need to take to resolve the situation? Who/what are my resources for the actions I need to take? If this situation is similar to ones that have stressed me out in the past, what am I doing to create these situations?"

Take the time to explore and evaluate what your options are. Because humans are habitual creatures, we usually need to prod ourselves to look for novel solutions. If the situation that is causing you stress is similar to ones that you've gotten caught in in the past, you do not want to use the same old solution. Generate as many possible solutions as you can. Once you have evaluated the possibilities and used your rational judgment to select one, implement the solution.

As you do the assessment and find positive, useful potentials, your stress level will be reduced. You'll stop feeling victimized and helpless and trapped. You may even start to feel grateful for the new opportunities you are finding or creating and you can begin to take pride in how effectively you are coping with the situation.

The final phase is **RESULTS**. By now you have a much clearer picture of the results you want. You've shifted your focus from the stressor to the results you want. You've stopped the flood of negative emotion and are now free to visualize yourself realizing a positive outcome. You've demonstrated your capacity for mastery of yourself and increased your coping skills.

Evaluate the results you are getting. If they are still not where you want them, experiment with tweaking what you are doing. Be patient, it usually takes time to reverse stressful situations. In the meantime, choose to see whatever it is that you are dealing with as a situation that will bring you benefit. Relax and allow your life to evolve. One of the best stress reduction strategies I know is to resolve to stay relaxed and calm and to course-correct and relax when I find myself getting tense.

Tony Robbins (in his work *Awaken the Giant Within: How to Take Immediate Control of Your Mental, Emotional, Physical, and Financial Destiny*) says that the quality of life we have is determined by the quality of the questions that we ask. Most people ask questions like:

"When is it going to be Friday?"

"When will I ever be able to quit this job?"

"Why does everybody try to make my life miserable?"

"How many more weeks until vacation?"

"What's on television tonight?"

Negatively slanted questions often begin with "why?":

"Why is this happening to me?"

"Why doesn't my spouse treat me the way I deserve to be treated?"

"Why don't my kids behave better?"

"Why" questions are often "whine" questions. Whining is a waste of time and energy. It puts us in a negative mind-set. Positive results do not ever arise from a negative perspective.

A recent seminar attendee told me that her mother asked a ritual question every afternoon when she returned from school: "Did you meet anyone that you liked better than yourself?" Each day she said, "No." What a great question! Perhaps you could start asking yourself that question each day. If you don't answer "No" that's a signal that you should continue the remodeling and redecorating of your psyche and soul until you do.

Tony's advice is to raise the quality of the questions you ask. When I first learned about the technique, I developed an early morning question. It was "What can I do to make today productive and happy?" Asking that question meant, I'd go around all day looking for things to make me feel productive and happy. My life was happier and less stressful.

Other questions that Tony suggested were:

"What's great about this situation?"

"What can I learn here?"

"What am I willing to do to fix this?"

"What am I not willing to do to fix this?"

These questions do the same thing for you that Alden's photography class did for him—teach you to look from another perspective. When you change your perspective, you change your world. There are two kinds of people on this earth; those who see the silver lining in the clouds and those who see the clouds in the silver linings. You get to choose.

Action Steps

1. Give yourself a breath break every hour. Stop your activity, inhale deeply and fully, then slowly exhale. Repeat 3 - 4 times and then return to your activity.
2. Give yourself 2 - 3 hours every week when you are answering no one except yourself. Do whatever it is that pleases you most.
3. Take a mini-mind vacation. Close your eyes, breathe deeply, and imagine yourself in your favorite spot in the world. Allow yourself to see, hear, smell, and feel the sensations of the place. Visit briefly and return to the "real world."
4. Enjoy a hot shower, bath, sauna, or Jacuzzi. Anything warm tends to be relaxing.
5. Use stopped-at-a-traffic-light time to stretch. Roll your neck forward to rest on your chest, stretch your arms and legs as far as you can. Play with the idea of coming up with as many different moves as you possibly can for car stretching. Obviously, only do this when you are stopped.
6. When you are feeling angry, upset, or stressed-out, ask yourself if there is another emotion you could choose to feel instead.

Points to Ponder

- When you are angry at the world, or yourself, don't turn on those closest to you. Turn to them.
- Remember, being angry is a choice. You can always choose not to be angry.
- Once you see the world differently, the world is different.
- Happiness is a choice.
- Any pain, negativity, or anger inside of you occupies space that could be filled with joy.
- Being in conflict is a choice.
- A thought can change your life.
- The cosmic radio station constantly broadcasts on WSAD or WJOY. Each of us chooses where we tune in.

Chapter 10

THE MOTIVACTION PLAN: HOW TO GET WHAT YOU WANT

I HAD BEEN DOING *Olympic distance triathlons for a couple of years. Olympic distance races are swim - 1 mile, bike - 25 miles, and run - 6.2 miles. Some of the mystery and excitement had gone from the experience. Barring mechanical problems or flat tires during the bike ride, I knew I would finish each race and could quite accurately predict my finishing times.*

One day a tiny question fluttered against my consciousness, "Could you do an Ironman?" I let it go. The question arose again—and again. Each time, the impression it made was louder and more distinct. I kept dismissing it and it kept returning. One day the decision was made. If I was to find out if I could do it, I was going to have to do sign up for one and go for it. I got out the application, filled it out, wrote a check, and sent it off. I was going to find out if I had the strength, stamina, and skill, to swim 2.4 miles, bicycle 112 miles, and run a full marathon, 26 miles, 285 yards.

At the time I made the decision the longest run I had ever done was about 10 miles. I had never swum more than a mile. Fifty miles was my maximum bike ride. I didn't have a clue as to what the experience would really be like. The decision to do an Ironman was a leap—a huge leap!

I had about four months to train for the race which was going to be held on Cape Cod shortly after Labor Day. The summer was spent training. Training was intermingled with my responsibilities as a parent, maintaining the household, occasionally helping my husband in his business and attempting, at times, to work on my dissertation. Training became a big focus. Most days I tried to do two workouts per day. I might run in the morning and cycle in the afternoon. Other days I'd ride my bicycle to the pond, swim, and cycle home. I found another woman who was planning to do the same race, and we became training partners. Particularly on those long bike rides, it was wonderful to have company. My body responded to the training; I could feel the increased strength and endurance building as the summer progressed.

As the summer progressed, I could feel my emotions building as well. They vacillated between eagerness and pure terror! There were times when I felt so confident and strong and sure. I was anticipating the challenge of the race with great eagerness. Waiting for the race took on some of the aura of being a child and waiting for Christmas. The flip side of the confidence was anxiety, big-time anxiety! I'd say things to myself like, "You're crazy! What are you doing this for? You paid them money to do this?!"

I found that I could center myself by asking, "Rita, what is the worst thing that will happen?" The worst thing would be that I'd drown in the swim—the swim part of the race was the most psychologically challenging for me. I knew that there would be lifeguards and boats strung out all along the course. I was much more likely to drown during one of my training swims. Besides that, I was a strong swimmer.

"So, what's the next worst outcome?" The next worst outcome would be that I'd get hurt during the race. I was training and building up my strength. I was sensible and made the commitment to monitor my body during the race and drop out if I was having pain that would preclude my finishing. "And the next worst outcome?" I would discover that I couldn't finish the race. "And the result of that?" I'd learn what I needed to do differently the next time in order to be successful. I had nothing to lose by continuing with my plan to do the race.

During that summer, whenever the emotion rose and got in my way, I'd go through the process to get my reasoning back on top of my emotion. Then I'd deliberately switch my thoughts to the fun and excitement of doing the race. I visualized about what it would be like to cross the finish line. That was a process that psyched me up! It turned me on! It provided the energy to train when the weather was hot, or I felt tired, or I just didn't have the enthusiasm for yet another run.

Race weekend arrived. The anxiety and tension rose to a higher level than ever. As I drove to the Cape, I thought about the race and felt daunted by the enormity of the goal I had set. The questions "What will it be like? Can I do it?" rolled over and over in my mind, making it difficult to focus on driving. I was so relieved when I arrived at the carbo load dinner and found that almost everyone else was as anxious as I. A vigorous, energetic and charming Johnny Kelley, the marathoner then is his eighties, was the guest starter for the race. He came into the dining room singing, When Irish Eyes Are Smiling. His wonderful presence was moving. What a role model and example of the reality that, although we all get older, we don't have to age.

As I went to bed that night, I prayed for calm water during the swim. I was calmer about the whole race, but I really, really, really wanted to ocean to be calm the next morning. Amazingly, I slept soundly. As I walked to the race start, I could see the water. Calm! All right!

Pre-race preparations went by in a blur and suddenly I was lined up with the other athletes, awaiting the sound of the starting gun. I watched Johnny raise the gun in the air, heard the blast, and was running down the beach on the first leg of a long day's journey. Later, I heard that Johnny had remarked as he watched us run into the water, "There go the real athletes." Wow! An athlete of the caliber of Johnny Kelly recognizing me, Rita Losee. What a kick!

I felt great in the swim. About two-thirds of the way through the swim, I suddenly realized that I was swimming through swells that were three to four feet high. My glass-surfaced water was undulating. When I lifted my head to sight on the orange marker buoys that outlined the course, I needed to make sure that I was on top of a wave in order to see. If I was in the trough of the waves, I saw nothing but water. It wasn't a problem. I no longer needed to be concerned about whether I could handle the rough water. I was handling it. I finished the swim in one hour, ten minutes.

I rinsed off, changed, and raced toward my bicycle. Now just one hundred and twelve miles of cycling was ahead of me. The route led along the lower arm of Cape Cod, out to Truro then back to Craigsville Beach. What a glorious late summer day. Warm sunshine, low humidity, and little wind. A day made for a long bike ride. As I cycled, I ate and drank, knowing I needed to stay both nourished and hydrated. As we moved through the villages of the Cape, people on their way to church stopped and applauded. It was fun to watch the older women in particular. They would applaud and then when they realized that I was a woman, break into great smiles and raise the tempo of their applause.

About fifty miles into the ride, I came upon a fellow racer who had a flat tire and asked if he could use my pump. Conundrum! Did I interrupt my race to help him—or ignore his plight and pursue my own goal? Within the few seconds that it took to draw abreast of him, I carried on an intense debate with myself. I stopped and lent him my pump. Giving him instructions to bring it with him and pass it to me when he caught up with me, I was off again, heading for the turn-around and the peanut butter sandwiches at the aid station.

As I rode along munching my sandwich, I realized how much fun I was having. I was getting a bonus! I had come looking for the challenge and the joy of meeting a hard goal, but I was really having a great time. I tore the dry, dry crust from my sandwich with my teeth and spit it out. Then I started to laugh. I was having a blast breaking the rules. I didn't wash my hands before eating, I was spitting my food out onto the ground and not eating the crusts, I was wiping my hands on my pants. How beautifully uncivilized this all was!

Some six hours after I started biking, I rode into the transition area and racked my bike. Wow! My legs felt stiff. Off with the biking shoes, on with the running shoes. Now there was just a marathon between me and the finish line.

After ten to fifteen minutes of running the circulation shifted in my leg muscles and I began to run easily. The race route was flat, wonderfully flat. The miles ticked off. I ran down the one hill on the course, a very long one that marked the half-way point. And then back up. I was halfway through the marathon! "Hey, Rita, You're going to make it!"

Suddenly at mile twenty, my right knee started to hurt. The pain was sharp enough to cause me to stop and walk. It didn't hurt when I walked, so for the next five miles I walked. At times, I tried running again. As the knee continued to hurt, I continued to walk. Finally, at mile twenty five, I attempted, once again, to run. No pain! I picked up the pace.

Twelve hours and thirty minutes after the starting gun, I raised my arms in joy as I crossed the finish line. I had done it! I had achieved my goal and in the process I had become more than I had ever been before. I can't fully articulate the change that the experience of running an Ironman created, but a stronger, more capable, more confident woman crossed the finish line than the one who raced down the beach twelve hours and thirty minutes earlier. They placed my finisher's medal around my neck as I learned that I was National Ultradistance Champion for the year. Shortly after, I got a massage and then immersed my body in the hot tub.

Ordinary people live by default. They don't set goals or make specific plans for meeting them. Ordinary people don't come close to their potential or their dreams. They don't convert their potential to reality; they don't concretize their dreams to plans. You, however, are extraordinary. You are ready to "commit to it and go!" The MotivACTion Plan that follows is your road map to success —whatever it is that means success to you.

Brian Tracy outlines the following five goal-getting steps, taken from Nightingale Conant's *Insight Series*:

1. **Idealize**—what is it that you really want? What do you dream of doing that makes your heart sing and your spirits soar? Spend some time in your heart and soul thinking about a dream so vivid, so passionate that it makes you want to explode with joy just thinking about it. The vivid idea that you create is a seed. Plant that seed and nurture it. It can grow to bloom in wonderful profusion.
2. **Verbalize**—I have a sign on my bulletin board which says "What you think about and talk about, comes about" (compliments of Larry Winget). So much verbal activity is about nothing. People talk about the weather (that's easy, we'll always have some!), the sports teams (upset when they lose, happy when they win—why put professional athletes in charge of your happiness?), money, sex, and time (there's never enough!), and each other (humans *are* endlessly fascinating). Use your precious words to paint vivid word pictures about what you want. If you want love, talk about love, not how you lack it. If you need money, talk about having money, not how you lack it. If you want success, talk about your success, not how you lack it. The people who live by default may not want to hear about your wonderful dreams. Don't get upset by them. Just stop talking to them and find other dreamers to communicate with.
3. **Visualize**—The vivid mind picture you create becomes a magnet that draws you to the goal—or perhaps helps you draw the goal to you. See yourself as you will be when you've achieved the goal. Notice everything about the scene, the colors, the sounds, the smells, how things feel, what people are saying, how you feel. When I was struggling with my dissertation, engaged in a seemingly endless, difficult task, I visualized what it was going to be like to put on that brilliant scarlet robe with the three wide, black velvet stripes down the sleeves. I wore that robe hundreds of times before I actually put it on to go to graduation.

Each time I visualized it, I increased my motivation to make it real. It took time, effort, energy, and commitment but, eventually, I lived the experience of my visualization.

4. **Emotionalize**—If a goal is worth achieving, it is worth getting passionate about. Let the passion and the excitement out. Feel it, express it, live it. The world is full of people who live in the passion of their pain. Not you! Live in the passion of your belief in your goal. If your goal doesn't ignite the fires within you, you've got the wrong goal. A goal of any significance is probably going to require time and energy to achieve. If you're going to do the time, have a good time while you are creating it. Your positive emotion will generate energy that will help you achieve your dream.

5. **Realize**—The last deeply satisfying step. You did it!

THE DENTAL FLOSS THEORY OF HUMAN DEVELOPMENT

We talked earlier about how difficult it is for humans to overcome inertia and make changes in their lives. That observation led me to develop the dental floss theory of human development. Almost everybody has been told by their dentist that they should floss their teeth every day. My informal polls reveal that it is only a small minority who actually do floss each and every day. The typical person goes to the dentist and hears the message; *you should floss every day*. The statement elicits a renewed determination and the vision of sparkling white teeth. We leave the dentist's office, clutching our new toothbrush, our appointment card for six months hence, and a firm resolve to floss every day.

The first week or so, we are virtuous and consistent. We're meeting the goal, flossing every day. Then comes the morning that we are late for work. We rush madly about the house working at warp speed to get to work on time. Do we skip the shower? No. Do we skip breakfast? Maybe. Do we skip coffee? No. Do we skip flossing? Yes! Once the string has been broken, it gets easier and easier to not floss. A month or so after our appointment, we've become very sporadic flossers. And after two months, we're back to ground zero.

When do we pick up the floss again? Of course! When the dentist's office calls to say, "This is Judy calling to remind you that you have a cleaning appointment on..." On the day of our appointment, the dentist says, "You really should floss every day" and we leave the office full of resolve...

I've been telling my dentist for years that he'd get much higher floss compliance if he'd send random postcard reminders to patients reminding them to floss or had his receptionist make random reminder phone calls. It takes energy and effort to launch a new habit. Like a just-launched kite, new habits are much more vulnerable to the winds and currents of life than one that has been in the air and flying for a while.

I first started to run because a friend recommended it. I had been fooling around a bit with an exercise program but hadn't developed a consistent habit when George suggested that I should start running. I vividly remember that first mile. It felt like I was running halfway across the country. The next time I ran, it wasn't quite so hard. I began to develop a fledgling habit, but then life would interfere and I wouldn't run again until George casually asked, "How's the running going?" Because I valued his good opinion, those questions were a stimulus to re-start the running program. It took one year of stops and starts and periodic reminders before my running habit was really mine. After one year, the habit was self-sustaining and I no longer needed an outside prod to keep it going. As I have observed my fellow humans, that seems to be the way that most of us incorporate change into our lives. We move two steps forward, one step back, one and a half steps forward, three-quarters back, three steps forward. I think it's the exceptional person who makes a decision for a change, makes it, and never looks back. Most of us change more effectively by *evolution* rather than revolution.

THE MOTIVACTION PLAN

The MotivACTion Plan grew out of my understanding that it takes both motive and action to achieve anything of substance. Both motive and action need to be maintained at a high enough level to keep us moving forward, even if, and especially when, forward motion seems slow. The steps of the plan are:
1. **Decide on the goal.** A goal is not, "I'd like to..." or "I want to..." A goal is "I will do...by x date." A decision is a definitive statement of what will happen. Making the decision is the first step. After the decision is made, the commitment is made, again and again and again. Every time I put on my shoes to do a training run in the weeks leading up to the Ironman, I was making a commitment to my decision to

run the race. Every time I finished a long bike ride when I really wanted to cut off the last ten miles, I was making the commitment to cross that finish line. Every time a business deal doesn't go through and I pick up the phone and place the next call, I am making the commitment.

2. **Write the goal down.** There is much power in written goals. Make it a habit to write down your goals and place them where you will see them often. If you are really serious about flossing every day, place a reminder note on your bathroom mirror. Writing the goal down is a way of beginning to make it a concrete reality, of making the unmanifest, manifest. Writing the goal helps you create the power to achieve it.

As you write your goals down, check to see how and if they mesh with the mission statement of your life (you now have formulated a mission statement, haven't you?). If a goal is inconsistent with your mission statement, re-work it until it fits. You are creating unnecessary strife and struggle if you are setting mis-fit goals.

Once the goals are written, post them where you will see them frequently. I place goals on Post-Its and put them on mirrors, my car dashboard, and in my calendar. Seeing the goals will help you stay focused on them and not lose sight of them in the "busy-ness" of daily life.

When you write your goals, endeavor to make them **S-M-A-R-T**.

S stands for *Specific*. We discussed that in step one.

M stands for *Measurable*. If a goal isn't measurable, it isn't a goal. One of the worst bits of advice ever given to American youth was Horace Greeley's famous dictum, "Go West, young man, go West." Without a specific, measurable definition of the goal, how was the young man supposed to know how far to go? How far west was west? For your own journey, make it measurable. "I want to get fit," is not a measurable goal. "I want to be able to run two miles in less than twenty minutes," is a measurable goal. "I want to be rich," is not a measurable goal. "I want to earn a take-home income of one hundred thousand dollars per year," is a measurable goal.

A stands for *Agreed upon*. When you are thinking about a group goal, it makes sense that the more agreement that everyone has about the goal, the more likely the group is to succeed. As was previously discussed, there's a group inside your head as well. For an individual goal, make sure that all of *you* wants to achieve the goal.

R stands for *Not Reasonable*. Don't set reasonable goals. If you set "reasonable" goals, you will set goals that are lower than you can really achieve. Set the kind of goals that make you throb with excitement. James C. Porras and Jerry I. Collins, in their work *Built to Last: Successful Habits of Visionary Companies*, talk about BHAGs. BHAGs (big, hairy, audacious goals) are the kind of goals you should set. BHAGs are thrilling and motivating. They take us out of our comfort zones and into newer, freer territory. The actual goal that you set doesn't really matter as long as it, for you, is a stretch. The Ironman goal I set was a BHAG. The benefit I got from taking the risk, pushing my limits, and achieving a hard goal was enormous. I benefit from it today as I sit at the computer working on this book—another BHAG. I benefitted from it when I struggled through the dissertation process, reminding myself that I had proven I had the stamina. I benefitted from it when I faced brain surgery; I knew I could do hard things because I had done hard things.

T stands for *Timed*. Putting a date on the goal gives it a sense of immediacy in your life. The date also enhances our sense of commitment to it. My dissertation took years longer than it might have if I had been more committed to a specific date. Most of us get so busy and distracted by the tasks of our lives that we have no time for the goals of our lives.

A mechanism for increasing your commitment to a date is to write a check for a substantial amount of money. By substantial, I mean however much money would make you feel really bad to forfeit. You make the check out to an organization that you absolutely loathe. Give the check to a friend that you trust and tell them that if you don't meet your goal, they are to mail the check. Talk about motivation!

3. **Make a list of all the reasons why you want to achieve the goal.** If you have set a BHAG, it will undoubtedly take time and effort to achieve it. You will need to stay focused on meeting your goal. Knowing all the reasons why you want to achieve the goal helps with maintaining the focus and the energy. These reasons form the mission statement for this particular goal. Writing the reasons out also gives you a picture of how this goal blends into your life mission statement.

Project yourself ten years into the future as you do this step. What will your life be like if you achieve the goal? Think about your future if you don't achieve the goal. What will your life be like?

4. **Make a list of all the barriers to the goal.** I doubt that very many worthwhile goals are ever achieved without stumbling into roadblocks and barriers. The more you are able, at the outset, to imagine what these barriers are, the more likely you will meet them and overcome then. When I was racing, it was very useful for me to ride over the bike course a day or two before the race. That way I could plan which gears I wanted to be in as I did the hills. It also precluded any surprises like mountains rising up out of nowhere that required a lower gear. Knowing that the mountain was there beforehand meant I could change the gearing on my bike and be ready for the hill. The more conscious you are of the barriers and obstacles you might encounter on your way to the goal means the more prepared you can be to stay on course. The Boy Scouts are right: "Be prepared."

5. **Establish a routine for goal-focus.** Now that you are aware of the dental floss theory of human development, you know the value of a routine for goal-focus. Spend some time each day focusing on your goal. Use the time in the shower to visualize your goal achievement scene. Start or join a group whose focus is helping each group member achieve their goals. The world in general will probably not be supportive of your reaching for BHAGs. Remember the saboteurs? Too often, when others see you really stretching for an achievement, it makes them feel bad about themselves because somewhere inside they know they should be doing the same thing. They know that they are selling themselves short. That creates a cognitive dissonance for them—and the quickest way to resolve that is to have you give up your goal and live at the level they live.

6. **Break the main goal into sub-goals.** One of the things I liked about triathlons was that there were three separate sections of the race. As I raced, I enjoyed the completion of each one and kept a mental to-do list in my head. Swim/Done! Bike/Done! That left only the run. It was a motivator.

The Chinese proverb about the journey of a thousand miles beginning with a single step is a powerful reminder that the achievement of a large goal is the progressive realization of many smaller goals or steps. What are the steps that you need to achieve your goal? If you list them and order them in a time sequence you will have constructed a path to your goal. Make a drawing or collage of the path and post it above your work area. For this book I have a path of chapter titles strung out on my calendar. As each chapter was written, it was signed off in red, and moved to its proper place on the path. It was a visual reminder of my progress.

Another tactic is to write down the steps in a notebook and cross them off when they are done. Referring to the crossed-off steps is a good pick-me-up when you are feeling discouraged. Reading through what you have done provides concrete evidence of your progress. A steps notebook is also a good place to jot down your favorite motivational quotes. They are a helpful boost when you are on a long goal-journey.

7. **Make appointments in your calendar to review your progress.** You should review your progress toward your goal at least once per week. What did you do well? Where were the problems or slip-ups? As you look at the slip-ups, ask yourself, "How could I have handled that more effectively?" *You are not allowed to beat yourself up or say anything negative about yourself if you've run into problems.* Part of the benefit of going after the goal is what you learn along the way. Without the slip-ups, you'd miss some of your most valuable learning.

It is quite likely that you will see patterns to the slip-ups. Most of us are not very original when it comes to making mistakes or missteps. Most of us have our favorites that we recycle. Situations that gave you trouble in the past are likely to be repeated. This is your opportunity to go back and devise new strategies for overcoming the things that trip you up.

8. **Visualize the achievement of the goal.** See yourself as you will be when you have achieved the goal. Act as if you have already achieved it. You can visualize by getting into a very relaxed state, closing your eyes, and imagine watching yourself in the video of your accomplishment. See what you will look like and feel like. Celebrate yourself as you visualize. Another way to visualize is verbally. Create a series of statements about how you will feel, think, and act when the goal is done. Make the statements in the present tense, for example, "I am walking seven days a week for one hour. I am feeling full of energy and excitement as I walk." You can then record your statements and

play them in your car as you commute to work. Making the statements in the present tense is a strategy for enlisting the aid of your subconscious in pulling you toward the goal.

9. **Monitor yourself for negative self-statements.** *Do not allow them.* Become aware of the things you say to yourself and others. Most of us have a fierce Inner Critic (we'll deal with him in the next chapter) who has a litany of messages about our failures and shortcomings, how much of a failure we are, how we don't deserve to have what we want, etc., etc. Whenever you find yourself facing off with the negative self-statements, take an antidote which is a positive, affirming statement.

    You probably have years of negative self-statement training; it becomes a well-entrenched habit. Think of those statements as poisonous. They are. You wouldn't feed strychnine to your body. Don't feed it to your mind either.

10. **Celebrate your successes.** Write the successes down. Talk to your supportive friends about them. Devise you own little ceremony for completing a step. Buy yourself a flower or a piece of jewelry. When I completed each chapter, I let out a cowboy "Yippee," got out my red pen, and signed off on it. The celebration of the little steps creates energy for taking the next one.

11. **Once you have achieved the goal, set another one.** When you have achieved your goal, you will be more powerful, more capable, and more accomplished than when you started. It is true that we are either growing or dying. There's no standing still. If I stop doing yoga, I lose my flexibility. Now that you've stretched your BHAG muscles, it would be a shame to let them atrophy. There are other exciting and worthwhile goals for you to achieve.

Action Steps

1. Pick a goal you would really like to accomplish. Develop your plan according to the outline above.

2. Write out all the separate steps to your plan on Post-Its, one step per Post-It. Arrange them on a wall or bulletin board where you will see them every day. A good design is to arrange them in the shape of a flock of geese, with the final step being the lead goose. As you move through the steps to your goal, remove the notes Post-It, one at a

time. Removing the Post-Its helps create a visual reality of your progress toward your goal.
3. Write your goals on index cards. Place them in your calendar, on the bathroom mirror, or on the refrigerator. When you see them frequently, you stay more focused on them.
4. Join, or create, a success group, where you and like-minded friends serve as coaches and mentors to each other in achieving goals.
5. Create a list of all the things that you have successfully done in the last ten years.
6. Create an affirmation tape for yourself. Say all the positive things that you can about how achieving the goal will feel. Make the affirmations in the present as if they have already been accomplished, i.e., "I am excited and happy about living in my brand new home." Play the tape frequently.
7. Find a person who has achieved goals and use him or her for a model. If the person is dead, read what that person wrote or what has been written about that person. What lessons does his or her life teach that will assist you? If your role models are alive, ask if they will mentor you. If you are afraid to ask, please read the next chapter and then ask.

Points to Ponder

- Written plans are the wings you give to your dreams.
- A motive without action leads to nothing.
- Once we are really clear about wanting something and are completely clear about our deserving it, we create a climate where we can realize it.
- Attitude isn't the most important thing—it's the only thing.
- Stay grounded in who you are while you reach for the stars.
- "Follow your bliss" (Campbell) is the door to success. Persistence and belief are the keys that open it.

Chapter 11

CHICKENS DON'T FLY: GET OFF YOUR DUFF— DOUBT, UNCERTAINTY, FEAR, FAILURE

IT WAS MY SECOND day of rock climbing. I had signed up at Eastern Mountain Sports for a day of climbing lessons. Twenty years ago, I had a hard time finding any of my suburban housewife neighbors that I could call and say, "Let's go rock climbing on Tuesday." So, here I was walking into the cliff behind Joe, my instructor for the day. Joe was a handsome young man who had full appreciation of that fact. I could hear his thoughts as we walked to the bottom of White Horse Ledge that morning—"What did I ever do to deserve having to spend the day with this woman?" On my part the question was, "What did I do to deserve spending the day with this arrogant guy?" By mid-afternoon, both of us had changed our minds about the other. We were both enjoying the day and each other's company.

We came to a section of rock that went straight up for 10 - 12 feet, then leveled off. Joe easily climbed up over the face, giving me directions as to where the handholds and footholds were as he moved. He climbed out of sight, tied in, then called back down to me, "You're on belay!" I answered, "Climbing." Joe replied, "Climb away," the signal system by which we each were very clear about the belay being on and it being safe for me to climb.

I reached up with my right hand, seeking the first handhold. The challenge quickly became apparent. Joe is almost six feet tall. I am five feet, three inches tall. Handholds that were easily available to Joe were a major reach for me. If I stood on tiptoe and stretched every cell in my body, I could just barely get my finger tips on the handhold. Plastered against the rock wall, stretched to the maximum, meant that I had no ability to move my legs.

> Unlock Your Possibilities

When I tried to pick up my right foot, my right knee was immobilized by the wall.

I reached again and again. Finally, I was able to make the attempt to get my feet off the ledge where I was standing and onto the wall. I moved up—and fell. So, I tried again. I fell again. And again. I began to look around for other alternatives. I moved to the right, thinking that perhaps I could see a different method of approach. Joe's method was obviously not working for me. I fell from the right side, repeatedly.

Perhaps the left side would work better. I moved left, saw a possible solution, tried it, and fell—and fell—and fell. I decided that the left side was not going to do it either. There was a tree growing on the back of the ledge. Perhaps if I put one foot against the tree and the other against the rock, I could go up that way. No way! I fell again.

I had now spent several minutes doing pull-ups off the wall. My arms were getting tired, in climber-speak, "blown." My blown arm muscles felt like last night's spaghetti looks when you leave it out beside the sink overnight. I realized that I had come to the end of my physical resources. I hated to admit it, but I was not going to be able to make too many more attempts. In fact, I was just about to call up to Joe, and say, "Hey, Joe, I'm going to make one last attempt." Joe was not only an expert climber, he was a pretty good mind reader was well. Just at the moment I was going to call it, he yelled down to me, "Hey Rita, this is your last attempt. If you don't make it this time, it's all over. We're backing off."

I did not want to be bested by this section of rock. I took several deep breaths, coaching myself to get all the oxygen on board that I could. I shook out my hands and arms, trying to relax the muscles and increase the blood flow. I concentrated and focused. All my thought was directed at successfully getting myself up over that section of rock. I reached up with my right hand, then my left. I managed to get my right foot onto the rock, then my left. Now the next move, with my right hand, now the left—and in a few quick moves I was up over that section of rock!

It was not a thing of beauty. There were no judges at the base of the cliff flashing signs that said, "For artistic impression, 6.0, 5.9, 5.9." But I was up over that section of rock. I had managed to do it! I thought long and hard about that experience. I had paid $55.00 for that rock climbing lesson—and had received a $55 million lesson in living. I had learned that failure isn't the end. It's a beginning!

Every time I went up on that rock face and fell off, I learned something about what I needed to do to ultimately be successful. It wasn't about failure. It was about learning. That afternoon on the rocks, I got free. I got free of a very disabling belief learned in childhood, that it was devastating to fail. I learned that failing can be, and should be, seen as simply a source of new information, of learning. I learned that you don't really fail until you quit—that's the real failure. I learned that whatever I tried to do was a source of learning and growth, whether I succeeded or failed. It really is better to have tried and failed, than to have not tried—and failed. With the attempt comes the learning and the opportunity for a new beginning.

Unless they have physical disabilities, all human beings learn to walk. All human beings fail repeatedly in the process of learning to walk. Imagine yourself as a baby learning to walk. You probably spent some time observing people walking about and started to think that you, too, would like to be able to walk. You knew that they got around much faster than you did. You knew that they could reach things that you couldn't reach and, oh, how much you wanted to be able to see and touch what was up there! You also knew that your knees hurt from crawling around on them all day. Enough of this! You were going to walk!

You probably spent some time observing what the big people did, gathering information about the process of walking. Then, one day, you pulled yourself up on the edge of the coffee table and prepared to take your first step. You let go of the coffee table and started to move from one foot to the other. Boom! Suddenly you were sitting in the middle of the floor in your wet little diaper. What are the odds that you sat there on the floor and said, "You stupid little wannabe walker! What's the matter with you? Whatever made you think that you could walk? Of course you can't walk, you dummy! Those people are all big. You're little. And they have shoes on. If they let you wear shoes, you'd probably be able to walk. But why try without the shoes? And besides that, you've got this great big wet diaper between your legs! Of course you can't walk! Give it up."

None of us ran that number on ourselves when we were learning to walk. When you fell, you simply said, "Oops! Wonder what went wrong. I wonder how else I can do it." Then you stood up and tried again—and again—and again. Within a few days or weeks you were a biped, happily exploring the new world that had opened up to you and seeking the next adventure.

Another thing that none of us did while we were learning to walk was to compare ourselves to others. None of us said, "Hey look, Dummy! You are nine months and three days old. You should be walking by now. Your brother walked by the time he was nine months and two days old. The Jones kid across the street, you heard that she walked when she was eight months old. What's the matter with you?" The comparison to others, and always finding your self lacking, was learning that you did later. Indeed, your mother, engaged in the competition of "My baby's brighter than your baby" with the other mothers in the playgroup was already laying the groundwork for you to learn to feel bad about yourself. You began learning at a very early age to compare yourself to others and often saw them as more than you—more intelligent, better looking, having a better body, a better personality.

There are two possible outcomes to this type of comparison. You can deem yourself better than someone or them better than you. It's comparing apples to oranges. They, all of them, every single other person on this planet, are different from you. They've all had circumstances that are different from yours. Even identical twins who were dressed alike don't have identical experiences. Our experiences shape us. They shape our thoughts, beliefs, and actions. Our experiences are individual, our lives are individual. We do ourselves no favor when we look at others and say, "Susie had done x by the time she was twenty-seven. What have you accomplished at twice her age?"

What Susie has accomplished, or not accomplished, is totally irrelevant to you. It doesn't matter what she has done. Success, health, wealth, and self-esteem are commodities that are unlimited. There's not a limited amount of success. It's not as if Susie takes x amount of success there's only success minus x left for you. There's not just so much health and if Susie takes some, you get less. Wealth is not limited either. We think and act as if it is, but it is not. There's is unlimited money available—when we run out, we just print more. Wealth was more limited in the past. When wealth was gold or silver, or land and animals or factories, there were limits to it. But the new currency is knowledge and information. That is available to anyone and everyone who is willing to make the effort to get it. The same is true of self-esteem. You don't have less because I've got more. If my self-esteem is high, it doesn't mean that yours is necessarily lower. What makes your self-esteem lower is looking at me and deciding that you are less than I am in some way.

When my kids were little and they got into the sibling competition, I told them, "You are playing a game called 'You down, me up.' It doesn't work that way. Putting someone else down does not put you up." Where you are is related only to yourself. How do you compare with last year, or last month, or ten years ago? Are you making progress, achieving goals that are meaningful and satisfying to you? Are your relationships better, your skills, your health improved? Are you gaining in wisdom? Happiness? If the answer is, "Yes," it doesn't matter what the others, all five and a half billion of them, are doing. You will not be any healthier, wiser, happier, or knowledgeable because of what "they" are doing. You will be healthier, wealthier, happier, and wiser because of what you are doing.

The satisfaction we gain from comparing ourselves to others and putting them down is an illusion. It means that we are giving someone else the power to determine whether we feel good or bad about ourselves. Whose shoes are you wearing through this life—yours or someone else's? When we compare ourselves to others and find ourselves lacking, we always end up feeling worse about ourselves. This is never a good deal. It is not okay to do anything that makes you feel bad about you. It is not okay to cause unnecessary harm to any sentient being. You are a sentient being. It is not okay to feel bad about yourself when you can feel good.

Is it ever useful to look at what other people are doing? Of course, other people's actions are a great source of learning. If I look at my parent's marriage and decide they aren't happy together and that I want to be happy in mine, I can study the process and learn more effective techniques for building my own. If I am an athlete and someone else excels at my sport, I can observe and learn how to make my own skills more proficient. If someone creates new knowledge in my field, I can use that to augment my own skills, and even better, springboard from that to creating even more knowledge. It is very efficient to look at what other people do and know and use them as a source of knowledge and inspiration. It is never a good idea to compare yourself and feel bad as a result.

You happily learned to walk in your own time and at your own pace.

You trusted your innate self and did what felt best for you. You didn't compete with, or compare yourself to others. You happily lived your own experience. There is great wisdom in that—happily living your own experience. You took your bumps and bruises. You didn't blame anyone else for them. You learned from your "failures." There is great freedom in conceptualizing your failures as ULOs—unique learning opportunities, for that is just what they are.

If fear of failure holds you back, if you are constrained by the possibility of failing, it's time to let go of those constraints. It's time to re-write your definition of failure.

Failure means to be deficient or lacking, not a good state! You never want to view yourself that way. There may be things you don't know or skills you don't have but don't ever label yourself as a failure. Let's redefine what those F-A-I-L-U-R-E letters really mean.

F = Forging
A = Ahead
I = I'll
L = Learn
U = Understand
R = Realign &
E = Excel

SILENCING YOUR INNER CRITIC

All of us have an inner critic. Mine is named Icey, which are his initials, I.C. He is male. I'm not sure why he's male but his name, Icey, suits him to a tee because his main function is to throw buckets of ice water all over my best dreams. He shows up in my head saying such flattering things as, "Who do you think you are?" "If you are such a success, why aren't your rich?" "Whatever makes you think you could do...?" He also says things like, "You're not very graceful." Sometimes he gets on me hard about my relationship to food. Icey has a pseudonym. He's also known as Icky because he looks like Jabba the Hut, except that he's a slimy green color. In sum, he's not a very pleasant character and adds no value to my life. I'd prefer to keep him far away from me.

It is never a good idea to argue with your inner critic. He always wins. As long as you counter with your defenses, Icey will up the ante. If he has to, he will go for the jugular. Arguments with him are always a bad hair day for your self-esteem.

A few years ago, I learned a technique for quieting Icky from Kathryn Cramer, the author of *Roads Home*. The technique she taught me to slow him up was to make a hand gesture and say, "All that aside, I've got just enough." So, if Icky is berating me because I don't think I have enough time, I just wave my hand and say, "All that aside, I've got just enough." I used this technique for a couple of years and found it to be very helpful.

Then I got to thinking about what I was saying when I said, "I've got just enough." I realized that I don't want to have just enough. I want to have plenty! I have modified Cramer's antidote for Icey. Now I say, using a power move with my hand, "I've got plenty!" I feel up and energized and Icky doesn't get to demoralize me.

FEAR

We talked in an earlier chapter about the way we allow fear to become a barrier to getting what we want. There is an acronym for F-E-A-R. It is "False Expectations Appearing Real" (we speakers love acronyms almost as much as government agencies!). We develop a fear. Virtually all of our fears are learned. We are born with two, the falling reflex and the startle reflex. Infants who hear loud noises or feel like they are being dropped will react with fear. The rest of the fears we drag through our lives are learned.

The things we fear that actually threaten our physical survival are legitimate. The fear you feel when your car suddenly loses its brakes is a legitimate fear. The fight or flight response which switches instantly on is just what you need to help you mobilize and cope with the crisis. Most of us fear far too many things. As the fears build up over a period of time we are less and less free. Most of the things we fear are based on beliefs—and beliefs can be changed. If there are things we want in our lives and there are fears that form a barricade which keeps us from having those things, we need to change the beliefs.

Chickens don't fly. Did you ever wonder why? There are lots of reasons that they should be able to fly. They are birds and birds fly. They have wings, hollow bones, and a body structure, which while not exactly aerodynamic, would permit flying. And chickens will fly for very short distances. But they don't really fly. The reason they don't is because they're chicken! They don't dare to really fly. In their chicken belief system, they don't think they can fly—so they don't. Most of us have chicken beliefs systems. We fear we can't fly, so we don't try.

Chicken brains are rather limited. It's beyond the capacity of their chicken brains to overcome the years of domestication and become freely flying birds. Your brain, however, is not so limited. You can overcome your domestication. You have all the capacity you need to overcome your fears. The only question is whether you choose to exercise your options.

In the 1988 Winter Olympics Eddie Eagle, the ski jumper from England, captured our hearts. Eddie was the least physically skilled of all the jumpers in the competition, but he captured our hearts with his willingness to take on the challenge. No one remembers who won that competition, but almost everyone remembers Eddie. We remember him because he spoke to our spirits, the part of us that longs to break through our own barriers and soar. We remember him because he reached out for goals that "should" have been beyond him. We remember him because he unlocked our possibilities. We could look at him and say, "If he can do that, maybe I..." We remember him because he literally reached out—and soared.

Eddie the Eagle would not have existed if the first time he had looked at a ski jump, he had said, "Too scary, Not for me." If you've ever stood on the ground and looked up at a ski jump, you know that it looks Intimidating, with a capital I. To stand at the top and prepare for pushing off and jumping takes courage. The process is deciding that you will do it; whatever you decide to do should be done rationally and thoughtfully. When you are about to push off, no matter what it is that you are attempting for the first time, you will react with fear—emotion. If you let your emotion drive you, you will back off. Not only will you have lost the opportunity to soar, you will have buttressed the belief that you are chicken. That will make it harder the next time you contemplate soaring. Poised at the top of your jump, you need to engage your rational processes again.

What are the reasons you are choosing to do this? You can refer to the list of reasons you wrote in your MotivACTion Plan. Is the danger in your head, or is what you are contemplating potentially harmful to you? There is remote danger in almost any activity we undertake. I could choke on a piece of my lunch sandwich and die, but my assessment is that the possibility of harm is greatly outweighed by the benefits. Are you "on belay?" What's your back up system? When trying something new, it's good to know what you will do in the event that things don't work out the way you want them to in the first place. Whenever we make an "all or nothing" attempt at anything, we've upped the odds that we'll be terrified when we do it. Remember that we don't think clearly when we are terrified; we're not sending oxygen to the cognitive parts of our brains. A backup plan relieves the tension.

When I made the decision to leave my marriage and the seminars, i.e., my income, went away in one phone call, I was scared. I was scared about whether I could make it and support myself comfortably. Remember my childhood had taught me that to be without money was terrifying. I needed a backup plan. My backup plan was that my parents are still alive, and the farmhouse on the coast of Maine was a place I could go with my computer under my arm and say, "Mom, I'm bankrupt. I want to live here for a while while I get my business going." My mother and father would take me in—gladly.

Did I want to go back to Maine penniless? Absolutely not. But could I do that, could I live with that? Yes. I left my marriage and have not regretted the decision once. I am learning in more ways than I dreamed of when I left to soar. I recommend that we all do fear drills. Just as we used to practice fire drills in grade school, fear drills teach us what to do, how to act, when we face fear. If you can fog a mirror, you are subject to fear. It makes sense to know how to act in the face of fear. The more you act even while you are fearful, the easier it will be. The more you face your fears, the less fearful you will be. You'll adapt quite happily to living in the skinny branches.

To do fear drills, just pick something that you fear and do it. The woman who fears driving into Boston can set a schedule to drive in 3 - 5 miles closer to the city each week. She can enlist the aid of a driving instructor or friend to serve as a coach and support. She can create a reward system for herself to help her keep her momentum going. And she can overcome her fear and give herself more freedom.

Another woman I know, a capable competent businesswoman, is anxious when she travels. She is anxious about sleeping anywhere but in her own house. Recently, she attended a two-day conference with a friend who shared a room with her. She was able to stay reasonably comfortable. Another fear barrier pushed back! That's doing a fear drill.

A secondary benefit of fear drills is that they give you the ability to say, "If I can do x, then I can do that also." When I was struggling with the writing of my dissertation, I coached myself by saying, "Rita, you can do an Ironman. If you can do that, you can get this dissertation done."

What you say to yourself during a fear drill is important. If you stand at the top of your ski jump saying, "I'm going to fall. I'm going to fall. I just know I'm going to fall and kill myself," you are literally setting yourself up to fall. As we discussed earlier, your subconscious hears every word you think—and believes it. Telling yourself that you are going to fall, either literally or figuratively, will make you tense and anxious, a guarantee that you will function less effectively. You need to tell yourself that you can do it and do it well. When you are coaching yourself through a fear, don't just say, "I can do it," say, "I can do it well." Invest some time in visualizing yourself doing it and doing it well.

After you have run your fear drill, spend some time analyzing your performance. First look at and celebrate the pieces you did well. Then spend some time looking at aspects of your performance that did not go as well. Don't ask, "Where did I screw it up? What did I do badly?" That's a set up for beating yourself up. It's not helpful and violates the principle of not causing unnecessary harm. The question you ask is, "How can I improve my performance? How can I do it better?" You then use that information to build your performance the next time—and to build your confidence.

My sister-in-law who is a nurse researched the effects of how nurses' comments influence patient falls. The issue of patients falling and getting injured in hospitals is a big one. Heather's research found that when a nurse saw elderly, frail Mrs. Alphonse doddering down the corridor, the thing she was most likely to say was along the lines of, "Mrs. Alphonse, be careful. You're going to fall!" That is giving Mrs. Alphonse directions, directions to fall. The nurse, an authority figure in the hospital, is telling her she is going to fall. Likely, she does.

When you are doing fear drills, don't have a "nurse" around who is telling you you are going to fall. Don't have anyone around telling you that you are going to fail. The people who predict your failure are toxic people. You know that you need to avoid toxic people for your own health and well-being. When you start running fear drills, you will create fear and trepidation on the part of people around you. Remember how we humans react when someone around us changes. Running fear drills means that you will have to confront your own concerns about how the others are reacting.

Yes, this means that in order to move past your own fears, you have to deal with the fears of others. You might as well be honest about it. Denial about other's fears and emotions is no more productive than staying in denial about your own. Talk to them as much as you can. Let them know what you are doing and why. Communicate how very important this is to you, to be in charge of your life and to live as freely and fully as you can. If they are loved ones, reassure them as much as you can that you love them and care for them, but make it clear that you intend to live, *really live*, as much as you can for as long as you can. This is, after all, your life. In the end the question is—who's shoes are you wearing as you walk through this life?

UNCERTAINTY

This morning my newspaper had a front page headline that read, "No Absolute 'Right to Die,' Justices Rule." That's funny! I thought that living, being born, gave us the right, indeed the obligation, to die. No one escapes this life alive. None of us know, unless we decide to commit suicide, when we're going to die. Even then, it's not a one hundred percent sure thing. Some people attempt suicide and live anyway. Life is uncertain.

None of us knows when we get up in the morning what is going to happen before we go to bed that night. None of even know if we'll get to go to bed that night. We try to live as if our lives were static and things will stay the same. Nothing ever stays the same! Sometimes the change comes rapidly. Your boss announces at 11:00 A.M. that your job is over as of noon. Your spouse decides that he's going to Tibet to meditate for a year. Someone gets sick or dies. Your house gets struck by lightening.

Sometimes the change comes slowly. The age lines start showing up on your face. The trees in your yard mature. The deserted old barn collapses. Mountains grow larger and then start to wear down. It all changes. The only thing certain is the uncertainty of change.

We try to live in denial of the inevitable stages of change in our world. We hate the idea of death. We attempt to live as if it's not going to happen to us. We give ourselves permission to live as if there were no life or death consequences to the decisions that we make. The reality is that what you choose to eat for breakfast is important. It is a life or death decision. You won't die immediately from a doughnut and a cup of coffee, but you will die—one little decision at a time. Unless you are suicidal and deliberately trying to overdose yourself to death on doughnuts and coffee, not eating healthfully is a means of denying the reality of death. It's also a way of reducing the quality of our lives.

We will live more fully when we accept the unacceptable—death. Acknowledging that today might be your last day alive would probably mean that you treat the day as if it were sacred. It is, whether you have one day left or several thousand. Becoming fully conscious of the uncertainty is a means of freeing ourselves up to appreciate the miracles of living—and of our own individual, wonderful, valuable, sacred lives.

The Alcoholics Anonymous prayer, originally written by Reinhold Niebhur, contains marvelous wisdom. "God grant me the courage to change the things that I can, the serenity to accept the things that I can't, and the wisdom to know the difference." When you find the serenity to accept the uncertainty of life, you become free to explore the wonderful world in which you live. You allow yourself to appreciate the small miracles of everyday, warm sunshine on a snowy day, the soft, velvet radiance of a rose, the sound of a child's laughter, the solving of a difficult problem, the smell of baking bread, or the sound of rain on the roof.

DOUBT

If as you have been reading this book and if as you have been living your life you have been taking action to change the way you think and act, you know that doubts dissolve in the face of actions. Self-doubts disappear as you try out your wings and learn to soar, as you confront the fears and move through them, as you allow yourself to believe that is it possible for you to live a life of freedom, growth, and joy. The more you allow yourself to believe, and the more you allow yourself to act in a manner that is consistent with that belief, the more you will experience the abundance of this life.

It is so easy for us to believe that there is not enough—not enough time, not enough love, not enough money. We were all born into a culture that believes in a scarcity mentality. The opposite belief that this world is one of abundance is becoming more widespread and more accepted. What we believe determines the results we generate.

As I wrote this book, I stayed focused on what I wanted, not what I feared I would get. I didn't focus on how much work it would take or how statistically small my chances were of writing a bestseller. I focused on the fact that I felt I had something to contribute that would make people's lives happier, easier, and more successful. I focused on what I wanted, my book at the top of *The New York Times* bestseller list. I programmed my mind to write it quickly and easily.

The process of writing this book has been an unfolding of resources that have just appeared in my life. I put in a lot of time during five weeks, but I wrote the entire first draft in that time. Later I told one of my speaker friends about what I was doing and my plans to bike across the country as my book tour next summer. She is an expert in media relations and she replied, "Now you've got to talk to me about how to get in the media all across the country," and promptly mailed me a copy of her latest videotape on media relations. While flying back from a New Orleans business trip, I was able to catch an earlier flight than the one I had scheduled. I was bumped up to first class. During that flight I sat next to a young man named Eric who shared his life story and connected me to his friend in New Orleans. That friend of Eric's became the publisher of this book. Coincidences? I don't think so. I believe that changing my belief from scarcity to abundance is making my life different—more abundant.

This is such an exciting time to be alive. Our scientific technology is giving us insight into the way the Universe works. That information is creating an awareness that our thoughts are much more powerful than we realize. The Bible tells us, "As your sow, so shall you reap." That makes inherent sense. If I plant corn, I'm certainly not going to harvest rutabaga. If we conceptualize our thoughts as seeds (as indeed they are—they germinate into the ideas and beliefs from which our lives grow), we recognize that planting negative thoughts—I don't have enough time, money, love, energy, intelligence—is not going to create positive results, i.e., plenty of time, money, love, etc.

There is evidence all around that the creativity of human beings is boundless. Look at the variety of lifestyles we have evolved over eons of time. Look at the incredible machinery and devices we have created to save ourselves time and work and increase our productivity. Look at the capacity we have now generated to create and transmit knowledge. All that exists around us was once a thought. Your thoughts create your world.

James Allen in a delightful little book, *As a Man Thinketh* (women are *not* excluded) written in 1910 tells us: "A particular train of thought persisted in, be it good or bad, cannot fail to produce its results on the character and circumstances. A man cannot *directly* choose his circumstances, but he can choose his thoughts, and so indirectly, yet surely, shape his circumstances."

More and more is being written about the connection of our thoughts to the energy of the Universe. James Ray, in his video-learning program *The Science of Success*, states that the unifying universal law is that everything is energy. The energy is always in motion and vibrates at various frequencies. Your thoughts are a form of energy. If I throw a rock into a pond, the energy created by the rock as it enters the water sets off vibrations that I experience as ripples. If I throw a thought into the Cosmic Pond, I'm throwing out a subtle energy that I can't see, touch, or feel. That doesn't mean it's not real and powerful.

When I first started learning how our thoughts influence the results we get, it was explained that we as beings are constantly vibrating. The higher the vibrations the more positive your results. My initial reaction was: "Bunk. Sounds like science fiction to me." The more I thought about it the more sense it began to make. What do we call someone who has a high level of energy? Vibrant! It's very obvious that we, as beings, do give off energy. Sit near someone who is profoundly depressed and notice how little energy you feel. Compare that experience with being with your most passionate, upbeat friend. That person gives off energy. We feel our own energy levels go up in response and then we give off more positive energy to the next person we see.

Does our energy attract things, people, and experiences into our lives? You'd probably quickly agree that our energy attracts or repels people. When we deem someone "attractive" we are making a statement about energy—the level of energy of our response to them and how we are reacting to the energy they are giving off. A growing body of scientific research is showing that prayer (thought energy) has a healing affect even when the person doesn't know they are being prayed for. A friend who's son was in a coma on the West Coast sat at his bedside for days, praying for his recovery. She reported after he regained consciousness and function that she could "feel the energy of the prayers" coming to him from the East Coast.

As a result of my introspections, I have become aware of how pervasive and ambivalent the attitudes of my family of origin were about money and success. I learned that I should strive for success but that successful people were suspect, that is, probably crooked. I learned that I was expected to get good grades but I wasn't supposed to "brag" about them. I think that bragging meant telling someone else while experiencing a feeling of pride.

Consciously, I was trying to go one way, while subconsciously, I was moving myself away from what I wanted. My family of origin also taught me that there was always abundant love to go around. I have never doubted that. I have abundant love in my life and it grows more abundant as time goes by. I was taught that money was scarce. I was taught that I should be self-effacing and modest.

Do our beliefs create our reality? I can't prove it. But I'm smart enough to know that I'd rather think thoughts that make me feel good than thoughts that make me feel bad. We live our entire lives in our heads, in our thoughts. No experience that I have isn't processed by my brain. Therefore, what I choose to think or believe has a profound impact on the quality of my life.

It becomes a matter of ABCs.

Positive **A**ctions
+ <u>Positive **B**eliefs</u>
Positive **C**onsequences

Positive **A**ctions
+ <u>Negative **B**eliefs</u>
Inconsistent **C**onsequences

Negative **A**ctions
+ <u>Negative **B**eliefs</u>
Negative **C**onsequences

As an athlete, I got better results when I took the positive actions, eating right, getting the workouts done, *and* had positive beliefs, that I could race efficiently and quickly, that I had the strength and the endurance to do well. At one point, when I was trying to get my run times down, I realized that what I was saying to myself and others was that I was a "slow runner." There was certainly no way I was going to become a faster runner when I was telling myself that I was a slow runner.

Doubts are overcome by a combination of beliefs and actions. Most of us don't turn over deeply ingrained beliefs quickly. It takes time, introspection and thought. Many of the beliefs that create barriers for us and are counterproductive in terms of our getting what we want are unconscious. Digging out the unconscious beliefs from our pasts requires that we look at painful, distressing aspects of our lives. Is it worth the effort? Absolutely! If you ignore those ideas and beliefs which are the infrastructure of your self-doubts, they tend to grow bigger like the monsters under the bed when you were a child. Over time, the doubts slowly erode your confidence, shrink your comfort zone, and eventually paralyze you. That is a crime and a waste of your life.

The way to tame the monsters of doubt, uncertainty, fear, and failure is to shine the light of truth on them. Like certain disease-causing bacteria those dis-ease causing beliefs cannot live in the light. The light of truth will cause them to shrivel and become powerless. The New Testament tells us, "The truth shall set you free." Telling the truth to ourselves and about ourselves is an act of courage and integrity. It will set you free.

Action Steps

1. Write down ten failures from your past. What did you learn from them? Write down the lessons and express your gratitude for having had the "failure."
2. Write a list of positive beliefs about yourself. Read that list at least once each day.
3. Spend five minutes writing as fast as you can, "As a child I learned..." Don't stop to think, just write as many responses as you can.
4. For each of the negative learnings in the above exercise, develop an affirmation that reverses the negative.

5. Learn to listen to what you say to yourself, very carefully. Are you saying negative things about yourself, either to yourself or to others? Using your awareness, break the habit.

6. Create a persona and name for your inner critic. Devise your own action and start practicing telling your inner critic (and yourself); you've got plenty!

7. Every morning when you awaken, make a contract with yourself that you are going to generate as many thoughts as you can that make you feel good and that make you happy.

Points to Ponder

- Failure isn't spelled F-A-I-L-U-R-E. It's spelled Q-U-I-T.
- Learn to like the feelings of uncertainty and awkwardness as you learn something new. It's a sign of life and growth.
- Our thoughts can imprison us; our thoughts can set us free.
- Isn't it strange that we often treat total strangers with more respect than we do ourselves?
- Fear is a choice.
- Take action and master the fear. Do nothing and the fear masters you.
- Your confidence muscles are like your physical muscles. If you don't exercise them, they shrink and grow useless.
- Experimentation can lead to two results: learning or success.
- The road to success is usually paved with many failures.

Chapter 12

INTEGRATE—DON'T DISINTEGRATE

I WAS VISITING *the Museum of Westward Expansion in St. Louis for the first time. By myself, I wandered through the exhibits of the artifacts and history of the westward settlement of this country. I spent a long time walking along a photo-mural wall, showing scenes from the trek of Lewis and Clark. Each separate photo of the journey was accompanied by an appropriate writing from the journal of Merriwether Lewis.*

Having completed the photo journey, I moved among tools and farm equipment and suddenly found myself standing before a crude wooden cart. Maybe it was the spotlights that made the cart stand out in such boldness or maybe it was the power of the cart, standing in silent, eloquent tribute to human courage, daring, and determination. I stood, unable and unwilling to move, staring at the cart and listening to it speak to the deepest part of my being.

The cart is very small with the bed perhaps four by five feet. The sides are simply small tree branches that were cut to length and topped with boards that formed a stable top. The hubs and the axle are made of wood. I studied the wheels for a very long time. I think that they are simply huge cross-sections of trees sliced into wheels. The tie is simply a hand-hewn beam which still bears the marks of the axe that created it.

I stood in front of the cart, humbled, awed, and overwhelmed by what I suddenly understood. The experiences of my childhood schooling had left me with the impression somehow that the pioneers who trekked westward were like a huge, mobile Boy Scouts on-the-march jamboree. I can't imagine how I got left with such a trifling view of such a prodigious undertaking. Perhaps it was the "California or Bust" signs on the Conestoga wagons that suggested that it was a lighthearted experience. In front of the cart for the first time, I knew the truth. The people of the westward expansion were visionaries and dreamers who possessed unbelievable courage, toughness, determination, and will. They were ordinary human beings who set out on an extraordinary journey and became heroic.

I also understood that day that some of the people who moved westward were probably carried kicking and screaming to the wagons. There were undoubtedly people, many of them women, who did not want to go. I imagined a scene where Jim came rushing into the kitchen excitedly yelling, "Sarah, Sarah. We're going west! There's gold in California! Me and the McDonough boys have signed up for a wagon train. We're going west! We have to be in St. Louis by the middle of April." I doubt that Sarah jumped for joy and shouted, "Yo! California, here I come!"

As the scene unfolded, I saw Sarah's shoulders slump and her hands twist her apron and her heart tremble as she thought, "Oh no! He's been talking about his for months. Oh, no! I don't want to go. My parents are getting old...And my sister, I won't ever see her again. I don't want to leave this house. There's that room upstairs where my children were born...and that little plot in the churchyard. I don't want to go!"

As I witnessed the scene, I knew that there were people who walked west while their hearts were looking east, and I knew that more of those people died on the trail than the ones who were excited and enthusiastic and singing, "California, here I come!" as they moved westward.

On the cusp of the 21st century, we are all pioneers. Unlike the settlers of the 19th century who deliberately set off in quest of the "west," we are all on the wagon train. The people of the 19th century could choose, or not choose, to becomes pioneers. They went to their frontier. We do not have that choice. Our frontier has come to us. The changes that we are living today are qualitatively changing the human experience, just as the Industrial Revolution did in the 18th and 19th centuries. The Industrial Revolution changed everything: where people lived, how they earned their living, patterns of family life, and how they thought about themselves. The Industrial Revolution was really an evolution compared to what is happening to our world; it took place over a period of 150 to 200 years.

What we are experiencing is truly a revolution, "an assertedly momentous change in any situation" (definition courtesy of *The*

American Heritage Dictionary of the English Language). The Information Revolution is creating momentous change in our total situation. Our world is irrevocably changing—and changing very rapidly. The current revolution is occurring over a couple of decades. Unlike our predecessors, we do not have a choice about whether to get on the wagon train. We are on it. We are all pioneers. Our only choice is whether to go west with enthusiasm and excitement, seeing the future as an exciting panoply of possibilities or whether we go to the wagons kicking and screaming. We *are* going west. It is in our best interest to consciously decide to walk with joy and follow our hearts as we go.

The successful pioneers of today are, like their pioneering forbears, people of resilience. They are the people who can face the adversity, change, and challenge of today straight-on and anticipate tomorrow with enthusiasm and excitement. All pioneers live in the skinny branches. There is no certainty, there are no guarantees. There never really were but people chose to live as if there were. Successful pioneers of any century face the trek with full awareness of the challenges and demands which lie ahead—as much as they can know. The wagon trains had scouts searching the territory just ahead. We also need to scout ahead so that we have as much awareness as possible of what lies ahead on our trail. The more we anticipate the challenges, the more options we can develop for meeting them. Successful pioneers know what to take with them and what to leave behind as they set out for the journey. The attitudes, beliefs, skills, and willingness that we pack for the journey will determine whether we find "gold in them thar hills," or lives of quiet desperation.

The Information Age makes extraordinary levels of personal development and satisfaction available to enormous numbers of people. Never have there been more opportunities for human beings. Never have the possibilities been more wide open. The ones who thrive in this pioneering world are those who choose to unlock their possibilities, those who accept the challenge of being responsible for their own success and happiness, those who find the courage to walk their own path. The demands of the pioneering path are extraordinarily high, the rewards equally so.

To be successful, you need to develop the habits of resilient people. You need to have a mission statement—a defining reason for your existence. You need to have goals which are consistent with that mission statement and behaviors that are consistent with your goals. It is not enough to believe in your goals without applying consistent action. If you do, you will live in a dreamland. It is not enough to have goals which are not connected to your beliefs. Without goals that are connected to your beliefs and core values, you will live disconnected from yourself. Your values need to be consistent with living positively. You cannot live well if you are dishonest—even a little. You cannot live well if you don't take care of your body. You cannot live a good life if you violate your spirit as a human and cause unnecessary harm. When you live inconsistently, when your values, mission, goals, and behaviors are not in harmony, you are disconnected—from yourself, and therefore, as a direct consequence, from others. You are shooting yourself down and selling yourself short.

In order to be successful in this pioneering world, in order to live well in this strange new land in which you find yourself, you need to be integrated. *The American Heritage Dictionary of the English Language* defines integrate as: "to make whole by bringing all the parts together, unify." There is no greater challenge in human experience than that of living an integrated life, of finding union within yourself. There is no greater pleasure or satisfaction than a successful journey.

The second law of thermodynamics tells us that things left to themselves disintegrate. I believe that that is true of human psyches as well. Vigilance, monitoring, and maintenance are necessary to guard against the decay and erosion that time and events will inevitably place in your path. We need to continually examine and re-examine our premises, to test and re-test our hypotheses. As humans we are given the gift—and the challenge of—conscious choice and free will. Whether you choose to use that gift to create a wealth of abundance, freedom, growth, and joy in your life is up to you. Choosing to exercise your option to be fully conscious and fully accountable for your own life unlocks possibilities beyond your wildest dreams.

When I close my speeches I always share the contents of a bag that I have packed for my audience to take with them on their own journeys. I'd like also to share the travel bag with you, the members of my reading audience. The bag contains the following:
• A book for you will need knowledge on your journey,
• A pair of running shoes because you will need stamina and endurance

as you travel,
- An apple because I want you to nourish your body and treat it well,
- A Gumby to remind you to be flexible as you travel,
- A $100 dollar bill because I want you to be prosperous on your journey,
- A rose so that you will remember to "stop and smell the roses." (A rose is also a reminder that sometimes things of great beauty can prick us and cause us pain. It is never a good idea to skip the beauty because we are afraid of the pain),
- An electric plug so that you will stay charged up—and current,
- A bottle of bubbles so that you will remember to play on your journey. The bubbles are also a reminder that sometimes very simple things are a source of great beauty and pleasure, like bubbles shimmering in the summer sun,
- A telephone to remind you to communicate and stay in touch,
- A packet of seeds to remind you that your ideas are seeds. Inside everyone of them is all of the information needed to create a plant of productivity and beauty. If you want your seeds, or your ideas, to grow and flourish you need to plant them in the right environment, give them adequate water and light, and keep the weeds from choking them out.
- A candle. Candles speak to me of campfires, fireplaces, and candlelit dinners, places where people gather closely together and share deeply. Candles are symbolic of the unique light that each one carries inside of us. Candles are symbolic, too, of the knowledge that each of us has. Each one of us could light our candles from another person's candle and that person's light would not be diminished in any way. So, too, we can share our light and knowledge. If we each share our individual light and knowledge, light each other's candles, between us all, we can create a warm and lovely glow that will transform the world.

I hope that this book has been, and will continue to be, a source of light and knowledge for you. Refuse to hold your candle under a bushel. Let it emerge into full expression, radiating the fullness of you, as you create your own life of freedom, growth, and joy. Namaste*.

•The divine Being in me honors the divine Being in you.

Chrysalis
A brilliant light obscured by shadows,
Sunshine trapped by dense leaves
or fog that mists the landscape with gossamer films
Layer upon layer of fictions,
omissions, and half-lies
Restraints, restrictions, limitations,
dim, diminish, choke the light,
shrivel the soul, still the heart.
Brilliant light longing for release,
a frozen brook awaiting spring.
Rosebuds hoping for explosion into velvet radiance.
A light tendril breaks free
seeking itself, seeking truth,
pushing through the pain, eroding the lies.
Truth consumes the fog, melts the darkness.
Clarity reaching inward for the light and coming home.
The river bending back on itself and drinking deeply of its source.

OTHER LEARNING RESOURCES ARE AVAILABLE FROM THE MIND AND HEART OF RITA LOSEE. Rita is a nationally recognized professional speaker who can help your audience expand their vision, accelerate their growth, and achieve their goals. If you are ready to unlock their possibilities, call 1-888-713-6487 or E-mail Rita at Ritalosee@AOL.com for booking information.

YOU MAY WRITE RITA AT:
Total Quality Living
PO Box 163
Boxford, MA 01921

"*Rita was sensational!...The audience was so riveted on her words, there were times when you could have heard a pin drop in the conference. But for me, what makes Rita truly motivational is that she is an expert by choice and experience. She obviously practices what she "preaches."*"

Natalie Timmons, Communications Coach

"*I often think about the wonderful program you delivered. The inSPArational weekend changed my life. I learned concepts, and met people that opened the door to my spirituality and continued self-improvement.*"

Jackie Davis, Digital Equipment Corporation

READING LIST
Adler, Mortimer. *Six Great Ideas*. New York: MacMillan Publishing Company, 1981.
Allen, James. *As a Man Thinketh*. New York: Barnes & Noble Books, 1992.
Benson, Herbert. *Timeless Healing: The Power and Biology of Belief*. New York: Scribner, 1996.
Biro, Brian. *Beyond Success: The 15 Secrets of a Winning Life!* Hamilton, MT: Pygmalion Press, 1997.
Blanton, Brad. *Radical Honesty: How to Transform Your Life by Telling the Truth*. New York: Dell Publishing, 1996.
Branden, Nathaniel. *Taking Responsibility: Self-Reliance and the Accountable Life*. New York: Simon & Schuster, 1996.
Branden, Nathaniel. *How to Raise Your Self-Esteem*. New York: Simon & Schuster, 1987.
Branden, Nathaniel. *The Art of Living Consciously: The Power of Awareness to Transform Everyday Life*. New York: Simon & Schuster, 1997.

Bridges, William. *Transitions: Making Sense of Life's Changes*. Reading, MA: Addison-Wesley, 1980.

Cameron, Julia. *The Artist's Way*. New York: G.P. Putnam's Sons, 1992.

Canfield, Jack & Hansen, Mark Victor. *The Alladin Factor*. New York: Berkley Books, 1995.

Chopra, Deepak. *Ageless Body, Timeless Mind*. New York: Harmony Books, 1993.

Chopra, Deepak. *Creating Affluence: Wealth Consciousness in the Field of All Possibilities*. San Rafael, CA: Amber-Allen Publishing Company, 1995.

Chopra, Deepak. *The Way of the Wizard: Twenty Spiritual Lessons for Creating the Life You Want*. New York: Harmony Books, 1995.

Cornyn-Selby, Alyce. *Procrastinator's Success Kit: How to Get What You Really Want from Yourself*. Portland, OR: Beynch Press, 1986.

Cramer, Kathryn D., *Roads Home: Seven Pathways to Midlife Wisdom*. New York: William Morrow & Company, 1995.

Csikszentmihalyi, Mihaly. *Flow: The Psychology of Optimal Experience*. New York: Harper & Row, Publishers, 1990.

Dyer, Wayne. *Manifest Your Destiny*. New York: HarperCollins, 1997.

Estés, Dr. Clarissa Pinkola. *Women Who Run with the Wolves: Myths and Stories of the Wild Woman Stereotype*. New York: Ballantine Books, 1992.

Helmstetter, Shad. *What to Say When You Talk to Yourself*. New York: Pocket Books, 1982.

Helmstetter, Shad. *You Can Excel in Times of Change*. New York: Pocket Books, 1991.

Losee, Rita H. *The Waist Management Playbook: All the Moves You Need to Make to Lose Fat, Get Fit, and Stay Thin Forever*. Dubuque, IA. Kendall/Hunt, 1994.

Jeffers, Susan. *End the Struggle and Dance with Life: How to Build Yourself Up When the World Gets You Down*. New York: St. Martin's Press, 1996.

John-Roger & McWilliams, Peter. *Do It! Let's Get Off Our Buts*. Los Angeles: Prelude Press, 1991.

John-Roger & McWilliams, Peter. *Wealth 101: Getting What You Want – Enjoying What You've Got*. Los Angeles: Prelude Press, 1992.

John-Roger & McWilliams, Peter. *You Can't Afford the Luxury of a Negative Thought*. Los Angeles: Prelude Press, 1991.

Olssen, Erik. *12 Steps to Mastering the Winds of Change*. New York: Rawson Associates, 1993.

Orman, Suze. *The Nine Steps to Financial Freedom: Practical & Spiritual Steps So You Can Stop Worrying*. New York: Crown Publishers, 1997.

Pelletier, Ray. *Permission to Win*. Akron, OH: Oakhill Press, 1996.

Perez, Rosita. *The Music Is You: A Guide to Thinking Less and Feeling More*. Granville, OH: Trudy Knox, Publisher, 1994.

Pilzer, Paul Zane. *God Wants You to Be Rich: The Theology of Economics*. New York: Simon & Schuster, 1995.

Ray, James. *The Science of Success*. Lattoya, CA: James Ray International, 1-619-457-6909

Robbins, Anthony. *Awaken the Giant Within: How to Take Immediate Control of Your Mental, Emotional, Physical, & Financial Destiny*. Simon & Schuster, 1991.

Roman, Sanaya & Packer, Duane. *Creating Money: Keys to Abundance*. Triburon, CA: H.J. Cramer, Inc., 1988.

Sears, Barry. *Enter the Zone*. New York: ReganBooks, 1995.

Sher, Barbara. *I Can Do Anything I want, If I Just Knew What It Was*. New York: Dellacorte Press, 1994.

Waitley, Denis. *Being the Best*. Nashville, TN: Thomas Nelson Publishers, 1987.

Wolf, Naomi. *Fire with Fire: The New Female Power and How it Will Change the 21st Century*. New York: Random House, 1993.